Order

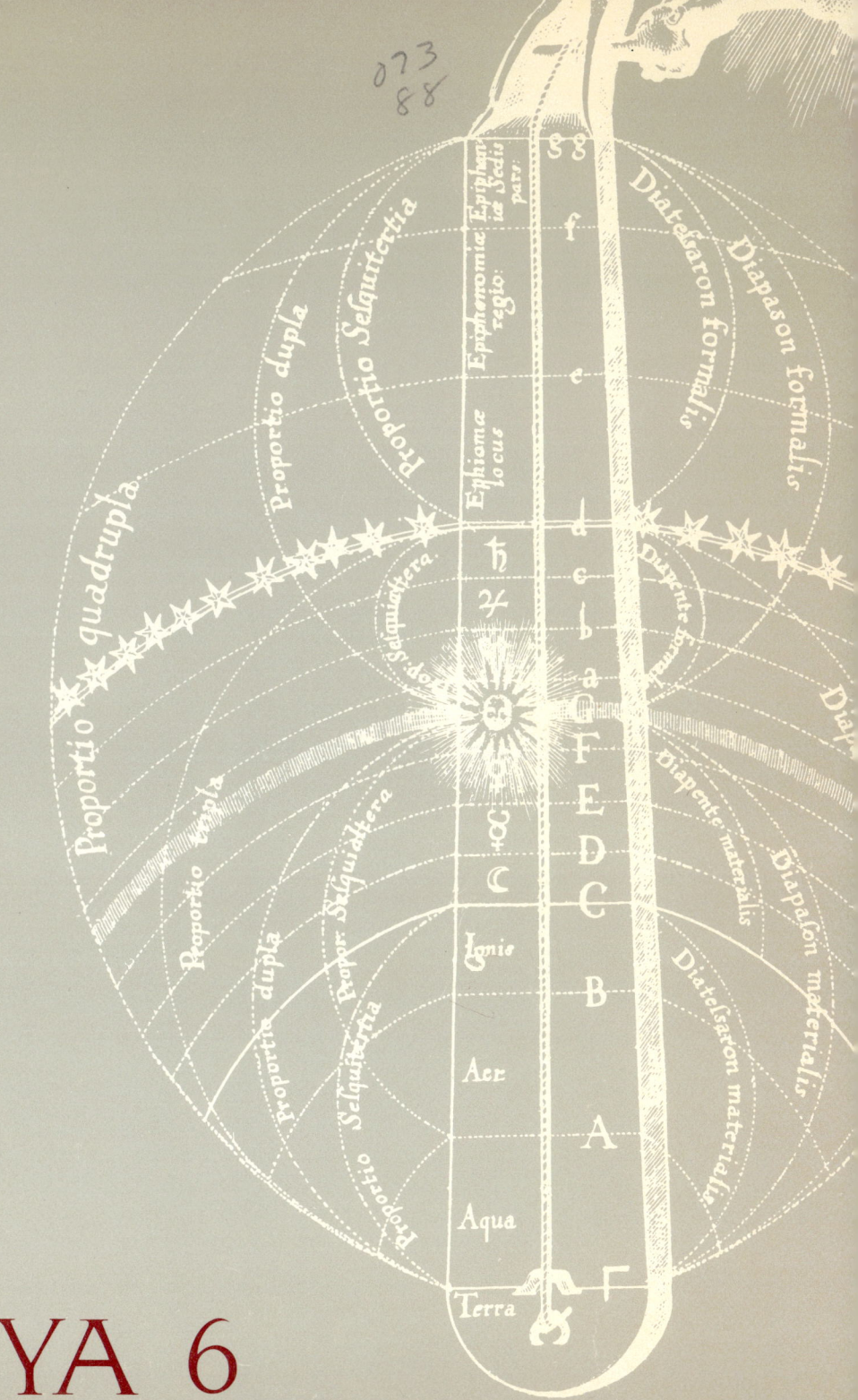

MAITREYA 6

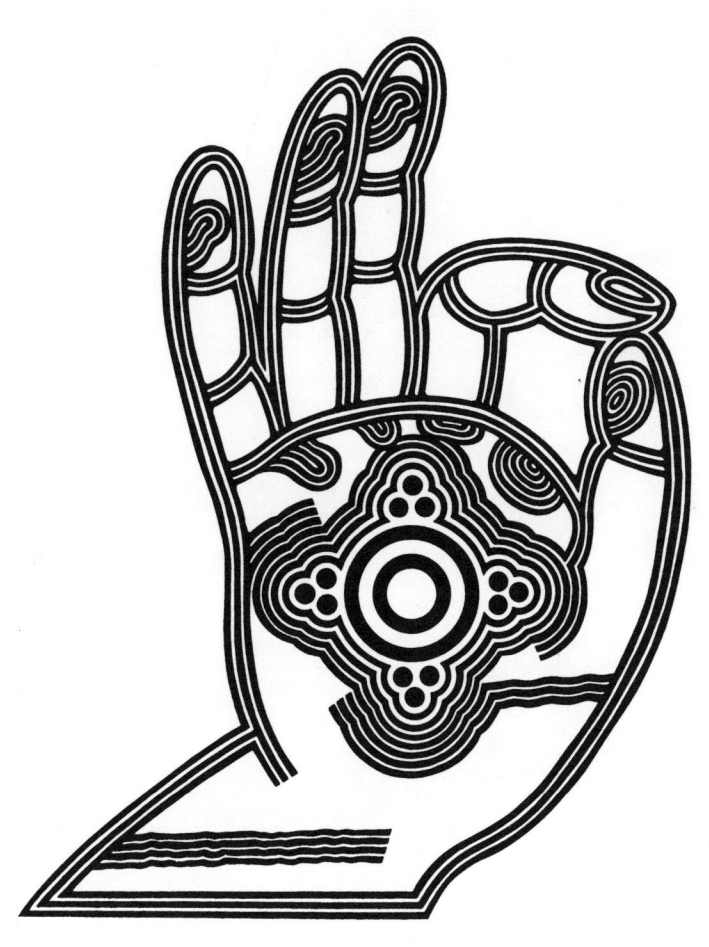

MAITREYA 6
ORDER

1977

SHAMBHALA

BOULDER AND LONDON

MAITREYA is published by
SHAMBHALA PUBLICATIONS, INC.
1123 Spruce Street
Boulder, CO 80302

Editor: Vincent G. Stuart
Art Director: Hazel Bercholz
Typesetting: HBM Typesetting Ltd.
Printer: McNaughton & Gunn Inc.

© 1977 Shambhala Publications, Inc.
All Rights Reserved
ISBN 0-87773-104-7
LCC 76-55122

Distributed in the United States by Random House and in Canada by Random House of Canada Ltd.

Distributed in the Commonwealth by Routledge & Kegan Paul Ltd.
London & Henley-on-Thames.

Printed in the United States of America

Acknowledgments:

"Thus Spake Beelzebub" by Henri Tracol © Triangle Editions, Inc. Reprinted by permission of the publishers, E. P. Dutton & Co., Inc. (New York) and Routledge & Kegan Paul Ltd. (London).

"On the Formation of a Psychological Body" by Maurice Nicoll from *Psychological Commentaries on the Teaching of G.I. Gurdjieff and P.D. Ouspensky* (Vincent Stuart, London 1952) used with the kind permission of Mrs. Jane Mounsey, the daughter of Dr. Maurice Nicoll.

"On the Double Origin of Man" by Karlfried Graf Von Dürckheim from *On the Double Origin of Man*. (Freiburg: Herderbücherei, 1973; Third Edition, 1976) pages 169–184.
Translated from the German by Graham Parkes.

"Spiritual Personality and Its-Formation According to Indian Tradition" by Karel Werner includes material from two of the author's previous works: 1) "Yoga and the *Rig Veda*. An Interpretation of the *Kesin* Hymn (RV 10, 136)," to be published in *Religious Studies*, (London: Cambridge University Press); and 2) *Yoga and Indian Philosophy* (Delhi: Motilal Banarsidass, 1977).

Illustrations pages 8, 73, & 80 by Jackson Hollomon.

Photograph page 64 by Zoe Brown.

Illustration page 104 Meditation-Ornament from the book *Urworte, Orphisch, Goethe* by Karl Thylmann, Gülistan Verlag, Stuttgart.

Contents

Vincent Stuart: Preface	page 7
Carolyn Rose King: Touching the Earth	9
Henri Tracol: Thus Spake Beelzebub	13
Maurice Nicoll: On the Formation of a Psychological Body	21
Mary C. Fullerson: Discovery of Intimate Order	29
Z'ev ben Shimon Halevi: Order: A Kabbalistic Approach	33
Karlfried Graf von Dürckheim: On the Double Origin of Man	43
Herbert V. Guenther: Towards Spiritual Order	55
Jean Eracle: The Buddhist Way to Deliverance	65
John Blofeld: Return to the Source	81
Karel Werner: Spiritual Personality and its Formation according to Indian Tradition	93

Preface

THE intention of this issue of *Maitreya* is to present the idea of Order as a spiritual system in which things proceed according to definite laws. Man has an organized physical body but no organized psychological body. According to one esoteric teaching, man is an experiment in self-development, and the only part of him which can evolve is his essence. This requires the awakening of consciousness, which has to be taught him by those who have already awakened from the sleep of the senses. For it is the contention of all esoteric teachings that man is under the power of the senses until he begins to think from ideas which come from a source different from that which governs our physical mentality and body, and to apply these ideas to his being.

All the ideas of esoteric teachings have as their aim the realization of man's inner evolution, although they differ in the methods taught. They have existed for as long as man has existed on Earth and are accessible to everyone who is ready to receive them. This occurs when people are at a stage where they wonder what is missing from their lives and feel a certain meaninglessness in everything hitherto experienced. This gives rise to a conviction that their own individuality, something which is truly themselves, has never grown but has remained latent.

Then the need for meaning, the need to know the reason one was born, the reason for the existence of humanity, the need to find the part of one that can grow, may become all-important. If we desire to find the meaning of our lives, we may realize that it is necessary to find and follow a spiritual discipline which will bring order into our psychological being through the development of consciousness.

Such consciousness as we have is fragmented and mechanical but is capable of development until it attains a level where "all is known together," that is to say, where a degree of unity is achieved. In the gradual process of gaining self-knowledge, by applying to one's being the precepts of an esoteric teaching, consciousness becomes aware of itself as the active principle of life, able to distinguish that what one has hitherto called oneself is but a collection of reactions to outer events and inner states, succeeding one another haphazardly. Consciousness reveals that one was without unity, without one will, without individuality, without consciousness, nothing but a creature of mechanical reactions, in disorder. Gradually one realizes that one's true self, always latent as a possibility, is the attribute of consciousness, and consciousness is the attribute of the true self.

It is hoped that the articles in the following pages will cast light on the ways by which man may bring order into his being.

Vincent Stuart

CAROLYN ROSE KING

Touching the Earth

Art is based on the simplicity of mind, accompanied by intelligence and warmth. To uncover this simplicity requires commitment to a discipline which reveals the complications of mind without perpetuating them. The student of art may begin to paint or sing or write for many different reasons, but ultimately he must work with the stuff of mind and its confusion, and in this process, mind must be tamed. This is the preparation of the ground, without which no art is possible.

Traditional art forms have understood the importance of the beginning and have placed great emphasis on it. The apprentice potter in Japan traditionally spends a year or more wedging clay and doing chores for his teacher without ever making a piece of pottery. Wedging is a process of kneading the clay into a consistent texture before it is placed on a potter's wheel, "winding" the clay in a particular pattern which removes air bubbles and structures the molecules of clay to facilitate centering on the wheel. The direction and rhythm of wedging are important factors in determining the excellence of the pot made from the clay.

Wedging requires practice, but it does not take a year to learn. The basic technique can be mastered in a few days or weeks. The clay itself does not demand that one begin so slowly. It is just there, with its qualities of flexibility and rigidity, an open-ended situation, just clay. The complication which demands a slow beginning is the person who would like to be a great craftsman, who imagines the beautiful set of dishes he could make, the art shows he could enter, the person who imagines how much he could impress his friends with his delightful pots, or who imagines the precision and simplicity he will learn while studying pottery in Japan.

For this person, a simple technique such as wedging is extremely useful in highlighting the basic confusion of mind. For while learning to wedge clay, one experiences clumsiness, the fundamental manifestation of one's fantasy world. Seeing the awkwardness of one's imagination brings the realization that one is obscuring what is actually happening.

All genuine artistic discipline has a similar beginning which might be called touching the earth, for it is indeed a grounding, a sense of "coming down" to make a relationship with the materials and the form of an art, and with oneself. As one begins to see the confusion that is there, the process also becomes a wearing out of ideas and distractions, so that simple attention can be paid to the task of wedging clay.

At a certain point, this beginning discipline becomes quite boring. One realizes that the person who wanted to be an accomplished artist is only kneading a lump of clay. That is all. It is not only boring but also somewhat embarassing, and one could begin to resent having to do this menial thing over and over again. Taking the act of wedging clay too seriously, it can become oversimplified, a stupid simplicity or frozen ground. But if one continues, even the resentment becomes amusing, and when a sense of humor develops, then real intelligence can begin to operate. The ability to experience the situation as both ordinary and ridiculous permits one to see that there is something more to the whole thing. One has a glimpse of how the first process leads into another, how one act implies the next, providing a continuity that has no connection to the original fantasies that filled the mind.

In order to understand this development of intelligence further, another example may be helpful. When a student has learned to wedge clay, he must then learn to center it, a technique of evenly distributing the clay on a potter's wheel while it turns at a high speed. An accomplished potter places the clay in the middle of the revolving wheel, applies water to the clay, places his hands on the clay, and it becomes centered. The whole process takes a few seconds. When the novice attempts to center the clay, it appears to be a battle between the potter and his material. As the clay bumps around the wheel unevenly, the student's hands bump and shake as he tries to produce a centered form. No amount of forcing will center the clay, yet if there is no strength in one's hands, the ball of clay remains wobbly and uneven. Having learned to wedge clay, the discipline of pottery has not been conquered at all: one is still stuck with the reminders of clumsiness. One pushes there, and that doesn't work. One presses down here; that helps slightly but the whole thing is still a messy lump of clay. Attempting every available strategy of push and pull is certainly necessary, for otherwise it would be impossible to begin. Nevertheless, the strategies don't work.

Rather than a theory or a new idea, what is required is precision and direct insight, which can only occur when one's heavy overlay of constructs become irrelevant. Having exhausted the possibility of any new approach, the willingness to nevertheless proceed provides the simplicity in which one finally begins to relax and learn from the situation. At this point the potter is able to respond to the qualities of the clay and to appreciate its responsiveness and thus is able to begin to center the clay. The boundaries between pot and potter relax, the sense of distance between the two narrows, and this provides immediate and precise interaction. There is no time to sit back and appreciate the communication, for one must be attentive and thoroughly engaged with what is happening. Relaxation thus affords an atmosphere of intelligence which is both direct and at the same time characterized by warmth, or communication. Rather than becoming cynical or self-contained, there is room for playfulness, which allows art and the artist to change. Warmth creates the space in which one learns without self-aggrandizing seriousness or frozen concentration, so often based on the fear of being laughed at or even laughing at oneself.

Wedging and centering clay are only a beginning in learning the discipline of pottery. The Japanese traditionally expect a student to work for ten or twenty years before making a "worthy" pot. However, this is not because the student fails to master the techniques of his craft, which can be learned in a year or two. The Japanese take ten years to teach this process so that the simplicity and the warmth of each act can manifest before the next step is undertaken. It is not only the discovery of simplicity that is involved, however, but equally the suspension of self-hatred and the student's development of pride, or dignity.

To understand the importance of dignity, it is necessary to look again at the frustration and embarassment which are part of mastering an artistic discipline. The process takes a very long time, and there is no guarantee that the next step will be easier or less painful than the last. There is no conquest of the mountain, no particular pinnacle or peak experience. Rather, it is a continual coming down, down to the ground, touching the earth. To make that repeated effort with both precision and warmth requires the surrender of one's territory of shame. One is so complicated and makes so many mistakes, so many warped pots or wrong notes, that it is enough to be embarassed. When one becomes ashamed, there is no space to breath, to move, to paint, or make a pot. An atmosphere must develop in which one is both embarassed and playful, but something beyond a sense of humor or relaxation is required. The student must manifest a pride that contains both gentleness and straightforward dignity, and which appears not only in the artist but in his art as well. It is this which is visible as both beauty and strength in genuine works of art and inspires one to speak of the universal in art.

When dignity and communication are a part of the early stages of learning an artistic discipline, they provide the impulse and the ground for the artist to make all the fumbling steps, and to master not only the techniques but the art itself. There is then something to be shared, something to be communicated, although the message is not self-serving. Yet one is willing to make the statements which contain confusion, embarassment, and also pride. One is willing to embody the whole thing, finally willing to get the complete message and even to be the spokesman for that message, the artist. It might seem a brave thing to do, but the message, although dignified, is a humble one, very simple. Nevertheless, to begin simply, to continue simply, and to end simply require the journey, the whole process.

HENRI TRACOL

Thus Spake Beelzebub

IT ALL began with a catastrophe.

Due to the "erroneous calculations" of some member of the "Most High Commission of Arch-Engineers Archangels specialists in the work of World-Creation and World-Maintenance," the comet Kondoor, when crossing for the first time our solar system Ors, unexpectedly ran against the brand new planet called Earth, and they "collided so violently that from this shock ... two large fragments were broken off from the planet Earth and flew into space."[1]

"Glory to Chance ... the peaceful existence of that system Ors was soon reestablished" – but certain measures had to be taken later to palliate the menace of subsequent "irreparable calamities" on a greater cosmic scale.

It is just at this point that we human beings appear on the scene. For it seems that the chief reason for our arising on Earth, as "biped Tetartocosmoses," was to manufacture by our very existence the vibrations required for the maintenance of the two detached fragments of our planet – namely Moon and the long-forgotten "Anoulios."

Moreover, fearing that, from the realization of such a slavery to "circumstances utterly foreign to them," these bipeds would merely wish to destroy themselves, the Most High Commission once again made a big mistake by deciding to actualize a special measure, the consequences of which, "unforeseen from Above," eventually turned into a "malignant sore," not only for this ill-fated planet and its inhabitants, but for the whole Universe.

This measure consisted of implanting provisionally into the bodies of these unfortunate beings a "special organ called Kundabuffer," which made them "perceive reality topsy-turvy."

And here is our curse: although some time later, the said organ, having been proved to be no longer necessary, was actually "removed from their bodily presences," the consequences of its properties remained crystallized in their psyche and were fully transmitted from generation to generation down to their remote descendants – in other words, to you and me.

Among these utterly unbecoming consequences, Beelzebub tells us, were to be found such uncontrolled tendencies as: "arrogance, the need to provoke astonishment in others, bragging, cunning, the vice of eating, egoism, envy, hate, imagination, jealousy, lying, offensiveness, partiality, pride, "sandoor" or wishing the death or weakness of others, self-conceit, self-love, swagger, vanity," and so on.

What to think of it? After all, while such a jumble is in no way pleasant to inventory nor easy to digest, as far as one is concerned as an individual, one could still live in hopes of finding a way to put up with it.

But there is worse – much worse. For sooner or later these "consequences" had to meet and to blend – consequences had to breed consequences, so that the resulting tendencies began to develop and develop "like a Jericho trumpet in crescendo" into the periodic and devastating urge "to destroy the existence of others like oneself," which meant wars on an ever-increasing scale, to the point of jeopardizing the whole human species.

* * *

This is our first approach to Gurdjieff's ideas, as they are expressed in the initial (and monumental) series of his writings: a dreadful, apocalyptic vision of man's fate in relation to the Universe, man's deep and persistent delusions, man's increasing loss of control, man's delirious propensity towards self-extermination. His lot is *disorder*, again disorder, more and more disorder.

Distressing perspective if ever there was one: all our beliefs in human capacities for endless progress, all our anticipation of a better world encounter here a blunt denial.

But had we not been warned? Did not Gurdjieff designate his "Beelzebub's Tales" as "an objectively impartial criticism of the life of man," in which his ostensible purpose was "to destroy, mercilessly, in the mentation and feelings of the reader, the beliefs and views, by centuries rooted in him, about everything existing in the world"?

So that from now on, it is up to us. We may refuse to go further – turn our back to this haunting vision and try to forget about it. After all, this is not the first time that, on the verge of disclosing the truth of man's real situation, prophets caution their listeners against mere curiosity: "Beware! This is not soft drink! – if you are not damned thirsty, you had better forbear..."

Now, are we that thirsty? Really able to swallow it? We are then forewarned of a new danger: "Don't be gullible. Watch carefully. Do not take anything for granted: wait until you have seen it for yourself. And this may take time, much time – a lifetime perhaps."

Are we that patient? Nowadays everything is prompting us to hurry. Acceleration rules all our functions, if we want to keep up. Indeed to try and be patient definitely goes against the grain.

Are we ready? Are we fully aware of our situation, and bold enough to try?

* * *

It sounds like a challenge.

Are we merely to accept Beelzebub's cosmogony as Gospel?

But, first of all, who is Beelzebub, according to Gurdjieff?

The Hebrew Lord of the Flies? One of Satan's lieutenants? A partner of "Arch-cunning Lucifer"?

Nothing of the kind.

When he was young, "owing to his extraordinary resourceful intelligence," Beelzebub had been "taken into service on the Sun Absolute" – the most central part of our great Universe – "as an attendant upon His Endlessness." And not only had he nothing in common with the Chaos principle, but he was a most eager defender of Order.

So eager, that having seen "in the government of the World something which seemed to him 'illogical,' and having found support among his comrades, he interfered in what was none of his business" with such impetuosity that he brought "the central kingdom of the Megalocosmos almost to the verge of revolution."

As a result, he was banished with all his followers to a very remote corner of the world – namely to our system Ors – where he spent many "years," according to an objective calculation of time (in other words, a good many of our centuries), in sincere repentance of his fault – until the All-Misericordious, on account of his invaluable services, granted him His forgiveness and called him back from exile.

* * *

Let us admit it: does this story not ring a secret bell in us?

Even if it does not fit in with our previous ideas about the demonic figure, it does evoke something more than the usual prejudices: an impression of tacit understanding and even of respect for his attitude, as if we felt at one with him, first in his sincere indignation and his immature but imperative wish to serve what he regarded as more right, then in his honesty to own up to his guilt, and in his full acceptance to atone for it.

"Errors of youth," we may think. But now that he is such a fully experienced veteran, are we not ready to sit beside his grandson Hassein and listen to him with a more genuine interest?

Grandfather Beelzebub speaks, and his tone of voice sounds so natural, so convincing, that we might merely fall under its spell and forget all our previous circumspection.

But the old narrator is on the watch, as if he were staring at us and observing our slightest reaction, and he takes corresponding measures. Until at times we can't help noticing some overstatement, or some deliberate insinuation, too obvious to be ignored, for example, when he calls our attention to the "excessive elevation" of the Tibetan peaks, which causes the atmosphere of the planet Earth to acquire in its turn an "excessively projecting materialized presence," so that at certain times it "hooks on, as it were, to the atmosphere of other planets or comets" and eventually originates threatening tremors or quakes ... And this rings like a discreet alarm, by which he reminds us to keep awake – for credulity, as he says, is unworthy of man.

On the other hand, we may catch more subtle vibrations here and there, in amongst his winding sentences, inviting us to discover some further meaning underneath, without which we would miss the essential.

Yes. For in spite of the author's "friendly advice" to skim through these tales "as you have already become mechanized to read all your contemporary books and newspapers" – which, by the way, is simply unfeasible – there is sufficient evidence that from the very beginning he also expects us to look for a better approach to Beelzebub's intimations, until we are able to "try and fathom the gist" of his message.

* * *

Will this help us to overcome our first impression from this account of general failure, of perpetual tumbling from disaster to disaster, of provisional and manifestly inadequate or insufficient attempts at redeeming the successive errors?

First of all, let us remember that in more than one ancient myth we are confronted with a very similar situation: at the very beginning something is missing, something does not correspond, something goes wrong. The first-born is a cripple, dwarf or Cyclops, a kind of monster that has to be slaughtered or metamorphosed, and so on and so forth.

There seems to be a doom on the very creation. Does not the great Demiurge endanger the mysterious Order that prevailed beforehand? The slightest change in the perfect Unity of the pre-existent Harmony is apt to engender all sorts of perturbations for which endless measures of compensation have to be found. Such is the unknowable riddle of that which is neither manifested nor "non-manifested," and which transcends the unavoidable contradiction between the principle and whatever its form of actualization.

But in *Beelzebub's Tales*, we deal only with the stage preceding the outer creation, when our Uni-Being and Omnipotent Creator found Himself suddenly confronted with the slow but undeniable action of the merciless Heropass, that is, the flow of Time.

Our Endlessness then "devoted Himself entirely to finding a possibility of averting such an inevitable end ... and after His long Divine deliberations, He decided to create our present existing 'Megalocosmos.'"

As a result, He was compelled to alter accordingly "the system of functionings of the two fundamental cosmic laws, called the sacred Heptaparaparshinokh (law of Seven) and the sacred Triamazikamno (law of Three)."

Now let us be on the watch! For at this very point in his narrative, Beelzebub gives his grandson invaluable advice, which could prove to be of tremendous significance for us, inasmuch as we are able to decipher it, to take it in, and to put it into practice:

"I repeat, my boy: try very hard to understand everything that will relate to both these fundamental cosmic sacred laws, since ... an all-round awareness of everything concerning these sacred laws conduces in general to this, that three-brained beings ..., by becoming capable, in the presence of all cosmic factors not depending on them and arising round about them – both the personally favorable as well as the unfavorable – of pondering on the sense of existence, acquire data for the elucidation and reconciliation in themselves of that what is called 'individual collision' which often arises, in general, in three-brained beings from the contradiction between the concrete results flowing from the processes of all cosmic laws and the results presupposed and even quite surely expected by their what is called 'sane logic'; and thus, *correctly evaluating the essential significance of their own presence*, they become aware of the genuine corresponding place for themselves in these common-cosmic actualizations."

* * *

Well ... once again we may find ourselves at a loss. It would probably take a lifetime to elucidate the real content of such phrases as Heptaparaparshinokh and Triamazikamno, in their unknown technicality.

Meanwhile, we shall keep in mind that, according to Beelzebub, we, as contemporary human "three-brained beings" able to think, to sense and move, and to feel, are still endowed with all the possibilities to assimilate and transform, from the cosmic substances that we absorb, the necessary elements "for the coating and for the perfecting of higher-being-bodies" in ourselves – that is, for the reanimation of such dormant potentialities that are meant to enable us to come closer to our real destination.

Thus, some objective hope is left to us: our doom is neither total nor final.

As a matter of fact, it was just to foster this revival and provide an actual support for these given possibilities that in 1922 Gurdjieff founded his "Institute for the Harmonious Development of Man" at the Prieuré d'Avon, near Fontainebleau. There, he made a point to prevent those who came to him, and who were already out of their teens, from falling into "the usual pessimism everywhere prevalent in the contemporary abnormal life," assuring them that "even for you, it is not yet too late."

It is not too late to try and restore the forgotten order to which our remote ancestors belonged, before the consequences of the properties of this damned organ Kundabuffer were completely crystallized in our tyrannical associative system.

"In everything under the care of Mother Nature," he maintains, "the possibility is foreseen for beings to acquire the kernel of their essence, that is to say, their own I."

* * *

"Not yet too late," perhaps – but not too easy, for sure.

Is not the leitmotiv of *Beelzebub's Tales* a constant call for "conscious efforts and intentional sufferings"?

Let us listen to what the author says in the concluding chapter of this First Series:

"Man – how mighty it sounds! The very name 'man' means 'the acme of Creation'; but ... how does this title fit contemporary man?

"To possess the right to the name of 'man' one must be one.

"And to be such, one must first of all, with an indefatigable persistence and an unquenchable impulse of desire, issuing from all the separate independant parts constituting one's entire common presence, that is to say, with a desire issuing simultaneously from thought, feeling, and organic instinct, work on an all-round knowledge of oneself – at the same time struggling increasingly with one's subjective weaknesses – and then afterwards, taking one's stand upon the results thus obtained by one's consciousness alone, concerning the defects in one's established subjectivity as well as the elucidated means for the possibility of combatting them, strive for their eradication without mercy towards oneself."

For a sounder understanding of this rather austere program, we need to realize that the second part of it is not at all an end in itself: "striving for the eradication" of our defects should not naïvely be taken in terms of "reclaiming" or "rehabilitation," in terms of mending our ways or seeking reassurance through aping any ideal pattern.

In fact, our real purpose should remain, from end to end, to *know ourselves as we are*, and this is what demands imperatively our constant struggling against our weaknesses, since all our ordinary manifestations are under the sway of suggestions that make us "reflect reality upside down," for the sake of supporting and perpetuating our self-complacency.

Now, to "work on an all-round knowledge" of ourselves means initially to make full acquaintance with the mechanicality which governs the entire network of our functionings.

And this, in turn, "is possible only as a result of correctly conducted self-observation," which implies the conscious mobilization and active cooperation of all our centers of perception and manifestation.[2] How much of ourselves, organically and emotionally, as well as intellectually must be engaged in this endeavour, we may surmise when we read that for a real study and experience of himself "a man must decide, once and forever, that he will be sincere with himself unconditionally, will shut his eyes to nothing, shun no results whereever they may lead him, be afraid of no inferences, and be limited by no previous, self-imposed limits," and he must be warned that to accept the inferences of such a self-observation and not lose heart he "must have great courage."

As a matter of fact, "these inferences may 'upset' all the convictions and beliefs previously deep-rooted in a man, as well as the whole order of his ordinary mentation; and, in that event, he might be robbed, perhaps forever, of all pleasant, as is said, 'values dear to his heart' which have hitherto made up his calm and serene life."

Is this not the reason why so many people who at first seem to be so keen on treading the arduous path of the ageless "know thyself" so quickly relinquish it? And yet...

"Such is the ordinary average man – an unconscious slave of the whole entire service to all-universal purposes, which are alien to his own personal individuality.

"He may live through all his years as he is, and as such be destroyed for ever.

"But at the same time Great Nature has given him the possibility of being not merely a blind tool of the whole entire service to these all-universal objective purposes but, while serving Her and actualizing what is foreordained for him – which is the lot of every breathing creature – of working at the same time also for himself" – for his own individuality.

"This possibility was given also for service to the common purpose, owing to the fact that, for the equilibrium of these objective laws, such relatively liberated people are necessary."

* * *

There comes the miracle without which no real transformation could ever materialize.

For one who "works on an all-round knowledge of himself," if he is ready to "shun no results wherever they may lead him," there comes the moment of truth. At the very instant he awakes and sees his situation for what it is – that is, objectively, almost desperate – a *reversal* takes place: instead of giving up the struggle, with his eyes wide open he accepts the challenge. He stands up as a 'man' and feels ready to try his utmost – because that is where he finds his genuine "raison d'être."

And while acknowledging quite clearly that he cannot dream of moving, thinking and deciding anything by himself he tries all the same, and *in the trying* he realizes that ultimately something is still up to him – and to him alone. For "man is a being who can do, and 'to do' means to act consciously and by one's initiative."

Truly, whether he wishes it or not he is bound to submit to demands "utterly foreign to him." But the ultimate choice is left to him: rather than passively undergoing the tyranny of forces that rule all his reactions, he accepts *knowingly* to play the game for the sake of serving, through them and with their help, a higher and meaningful purpose – thus restoring in himself the underlying order to which he belongs.

For this order is in no way an outer projection, but is the living reality of which he is the bearer, even though most of the time it has been – and still is – ignored, denied or betrayed.

To restore order means to liberate oneself from the spell of what *seems*, and to come back to what *is*. To this purpose, our tendency to lie and to dream, our passive imagination, our addiction to "what is not" and our fear of "what is," have to be conquered. Instead of yielding to our familiar phantasmagoria, we shall oppose it and free ourselves from it, thereby releasing anew the intimate flow of energy which corresponds to our deeper, essential nature.

We may believe that we understand this idea, but as a rule, we do not: we promptly reduce it to the nostalgia

for a "lost order" – whereas it is *we* who are lost, not order itself.

As a matter of fact, what we actually mean by "order" is necessarily limited, since it merely answers our craving for limits. And indeed, on the level of our daily existence, it fulfills perfectly its role of withstanding the constant threat of meaningless disorder. But there are other levels as well, other needs to be met, other menaces to be faced: against Chaos itself, against the Unknown, there is no safeguard. Sooner or later we shall have to relinquish our hope to feel secure: we shall have to take our own risk.

If we really wish to persevere in our search for truth and not be satisfied with any provisional shelter, it is high time to enlarge our scope and think in terms of universal harmony, which, according to Beelzebub, depends on the "mutual influence and reciprocal maintenance of everything existing," and implies essentially – in keeping with the principle of the Law of Three – a *reconciliation of the opposites*.

In other words, ultimately, this underlying Order must, in that sense, absorb, include and eventually assimilate all particular orders *and* disorders.

* * *

Now, in coming back to the imperative necessity for a man to disentangle himself from the network of countless suggestions and forms of mechanical functionings that keep him from being what he *is*, we may begin to understand why this renouncement, this "death" to all our "automatically and slavishly acquired habits" is the only key to a new way of life.

Thus the Gospel parable: "Except a corn of wheat fall into the ground and die, it abideth alone; but, if it die, it bringeth forth much fruit."

To which Gurdjieff echoes by another aphorism: "A man may be born, but in order to be born he must die, and in order to die he must first awake."[3]

"It is just this death that is spoken of in all religions.

"It is defined in the saying which has reached us from remote antiquity, 'without death no resurrection,' that is to say 'if you do not die you will not be resurrected.'

"The death referred to is not the death of the body, since for such a death there is no need of resurrection.

"For if there is a soul, and moreover, an immortal soul, it can dispense with a resurrection of the body.

"No! Even Jesus Christ and all the other prophets sent from Above spoke of the death which might occur even during life, that is to say, of the death of that 'Tyrant' from whom proceeds our slavery in this life and solely from the liberation from which depends the first chief liberation of man."[4]

But, strangely enough, our striving for this inner "death" is most effectively impeded by our basic incapacity, or reluctance, to maintain our look for any length of time on the unavoidable prospect of our own physical death – apparently for fear of losing all interest in whatever is meant to stir us up to action.

According to Gurdjieff, this incapacity corresponds to an objective measure of protection, for in the present conditions of existence the average man "cannot and *must not*" look his own death "in the face, otherwise he would 'get out of his depth' and before him, in clear-cut form, the question would arise: 'why should we live and toil and suffer' and he would merely wish to hang himself.

"Precisely that such a question may not arise, Great Nature . . . was constrained to adapt Herself to such an abnormality" and to take all appropriate steps.

Nevertheless, in so far as he sincerely craves for Truth, fearlessly awakes to his situation and realises his helplessness and nothingness, as long as he is reduced to his chimerical independence, the searcher may become worthy of opening to an impartial vision of his proper destiny as a 'man,' a lawfully conscious reflection of the universal order."

* * *

Are we becoming too bumptious? Indeed it may seem to us that we are now equal to putting ourselves in the position of such a high cosmic realization as Mr. Beelzebub himself – and this of course without ever losing an objective sense of proportions, nor the sense of humor which, by the way, he never parts with, even in his most bitter appreciation of the catastrophic "unforeseeingness" of our Most Saintly Cosmic Individuals, specialists in the work of World-Creation and World-Maintenance . . .

That is why, without relinquishing in the least our objective birthright to play our part now in the common attempt at the endless restoring of order, we may understand our impartial Leader when, in answering his grandson's question, he offers as his "last vow" to His Endlessness this ultimate solution:

"Thou All and the Allness of my Wholeness!

"The sole means now for the saving of the beings of the planet Earth would be to implant again into their presences a new organ, an organ like Kundabuffer, but this time of such properties that everyone of these unfortunates during the process of existence should constantly sense and be cognizant of the inevitability of his own death as well as of the death of everyone upon whom his eyes or attention rests."

May the All-Mighty hear this call! So that the remote descendants of our great-grandchildren may find, thanks to this most daring operation, more proper conditions for the fulfillment of their "Partkdolg-duties."

But as for ourselves . . .

Should we wait?

NOTES

[1] See G. I. Gurdjieff: *All and Everything, First Series, Beelzebub's Tales to His Grandson*. (New York: E. P. Dutton & Co., 1964) pp. 82–89, and passim.

[2] cf. "View from the Real World" in *Early Talks of Gurdjieff as Recollected by His Pupils*. (New York: E. P. Dutton & Co., 1973) p. 222: "Working on oneself is not so difficult as wishing to work, taking the decision. This is because our centers have to agree among themselves, having realized that, if they are to do anything together, they must submit to a common master. But it is difficult for them to agree because once there is a master, it will no longer be possible for any of them to order the others about and to do what they like. There is no master in ordinary man . . ."

[3] P. D. Ouspensky: *In Search of the Miraculous*. (London: Routledge & Kegan Paul, 1950) (New York: Harcourt Brace & Jovanovich, 1950) p. 217.

[4] G. I. Gurdjieff: *Beelzebub's Tales*. pp. 1232–1233.

MAURICE NICOLL

On the Formation of a Psychological Body

Man is given by the Universe an organized physical body which works, but not a psychological body. The physical body that Science and Medicine try to study is ordered. When a child is born it has this organized body that works in a marvellous way. The child is born with its heart beating, its blood circulating, with a digestive tube all ready to work, and so on. This really is a marvel. Now a child grows up and becomes surrounded by Personality. It begins to have a psychology. So we all grow but our psychology is not organized into a body. In fact, psychologically we are a kind of chaos as opposed to order. We have no psychological body organized or in any way comparable with that of the physical body. I mean the physical body is ordered but the psychological body is not. From one explanation of the further bodies we start from the idea that man is many "I's" entirely contradictory when he should have one "I" which controls them. This I would call a first glimpse of what second body might mean. I am talking of many "I's" as a man's ordinary psychological state which is not that of an organized body... Only through esoteric teaching and work on oneself does the formation of an organized psychological body become possible as distinct from the physical body.

All esoteric teaching is based on the idea that Man is not his physical body alone. A man who takes himself solely as his physical body is making a great mistake because there is far more in him than is represented by his physical body. The Work teaches that Man is given at birth an organized physical body and it is marvellous how the complicated physical body with its different systems, digestive, vascular, nervous, secretory, and all the rest of it, can be made in the course of nine months of our time. One thing you must agree with is that in the primitive original fertilised cell from which our myriad-celled physical body is derived there must be some organizing controlling principle that connects up to all its further divisions and arranges them in order. Yes – life is order. Nothing can live if it is in disorder. Here you are given a brain with its 2,000 million nerve cells. You are given a liver, a breathing system which can run itself, a muscular system, a digestive system and so on. And yet we take all this for granted and cannot understand the simple idea that life depends on order, which must have a higher order that controls it. Unless everything were ordered in us, from the highest to the lowest, we should not be able to exist physically on this Earth.

As I implied, very few people think about the miracle of existence, but simply take it for granted. When something goes wrong with this order in our bodies, we have to go to the doctor. An illness is due to *disorder* in the body. All illness is due to something not being in the right order, something that does not correspond to the fundamental order of the body and its different functions, arranged in scale or order. We can see therefore without much disagreement that order is a principle on which all living organisms are based. If they are not in *order* they die. The Work teaches that this order is connected with what is called the Law of Octaves, or law of things in order, or Law of Seven, the supreme example of which is the Ray of Creation. Here you apprehend things are in order, one below another, and all in continual creation. In the Ray of Creation one is

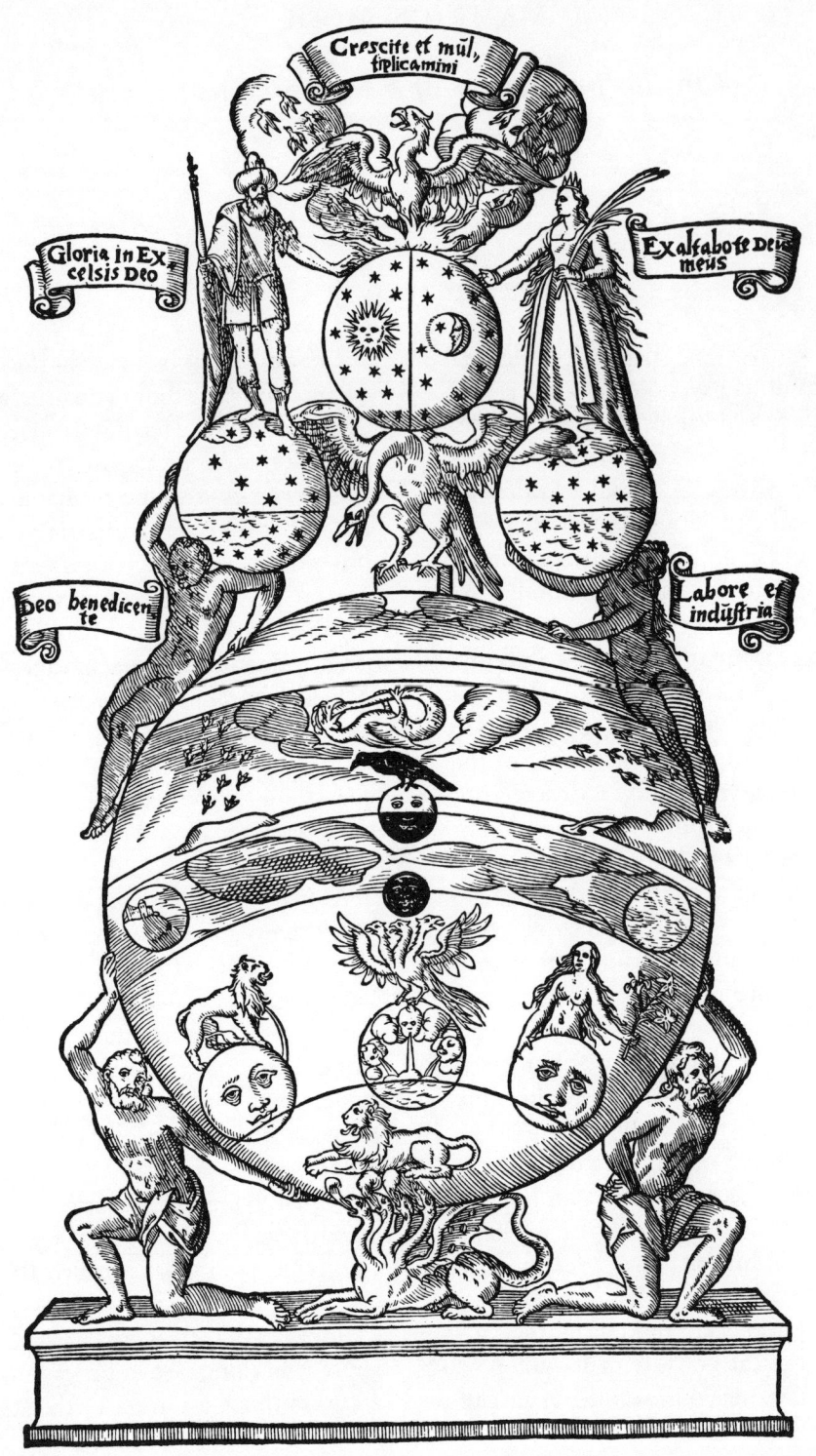

shown that everything descends by notes from the Unknown Origin of All Things, which is called the Absolute. The order of the body is therefore an octave, because it works. If the order of the body be wrong somewhere, then the Law of Octaves cannot work in it, because force flowing in from the highest to the lowest would be interrupted. That is, one would have disorder. Suppose, for example, that your brain were invaded by your liver. One can see at once that if this did happen you would die, because the brain is at a much higher level than is the liver, and the liver is again at a much higher level than the skin-cells that form your skin. Therefore all order is on the principle of higher and lower – that is, that which commands and that which obeys – and that is the fundamental structure of all living organisms. Even the amoeba, this little living single cell that we have to study in the laboratories, has structure in it and has a nucleus in it that has to control the whole and corresponds to the brain. But the body is not the highest in Man. In Man, as distinct from animals, we have a peculiar case. All esoteric teaching says the same thing – namely, that Man is born incomplete. He is given his body as are animals. There is in him something that he can develop, however, apart from the physical body given to him. Animals do not have this possibility, but Man has, so therefore Man is a peculiar creation. He can develop *another body* apart from his physical body. In which direction, or where, do the possibilities of this development lie? In what we can roughly call his psychological part. This is not in order. Man is given an ordered physical body as a gift, but he is not given an ordered psychological body as a gift. He must develop this psychological body so that it becomes organized in the same kind of way – i.e. through order, as is his physical body. All this Work is about organizing this psychological body, and indeed, up to the point when this psychological body, ordered in the right way, can not only control the physical body and its actions but exist independently of the physical body.

The teaching, in brief, is that Man, living in the given body, by his first birth, is capable of developing *three* further bodies composed of finer matters. But what does this mean and what ideas will help us to comprehend it? What, for example, might it mean that Man can develop *another* body apart from three further bodies? In what way can we picture *another* or second body? Now, we can conceive it first in this way. Imagine one man standing behind another man and controlling him in everything he does or says. The man in front obeys the instructions of the man behind him. That is, the intelligence and will of the man behind controls the actions of the man in front. We can take the man in front as the first body and the man behind as another or *second* body – that is, we can gain the idea of the second body *controlling* the first. This is easy enough to understand, for in any organization in life, as a military or business organization, there must be some degree of control of one individual by another in a higher position. In the case of a single individual, it is more difficult to grasp.

What in a single individual is going to control *what* in him? Indeed, it is impossible to understand, as long as a man takes himself as *one* – that is, as long as he believes that that which thinks, speaks, acts, feels, loves and hates in him is always one and the same thing. Now you know that there is a phrase in the Work which says that *unless a man divides himself into two, into an observing and an observed side, he can never shift from where he is.* This is the starting point of all else. It is actually the starting point of *another body* in the sense that unless this division begins in a man, unless he can become the subject of his own observation, nothing can ever develop in him that can eventually control him internally and make the outer *man-machine* obey. That is, no second body can be organized in him. Let us note here that the position of Observing "I" is always *internal* to what it observes. . . .

As self-observation becomes *deeper*, more *emotional*, more *real* and more *necessary* the position of Observing "I" becomes more internal. Self-Observation ceases to be superficial. Now around Observing "I" gather all those "I's" in a man that wish to work and bring about order in the house that man is. This forms what is called *Deputy-Steward*. The position of Deputy-Steward is therefore *internal* to the superficial man, the man turned to life and driven by outer circumstances.... Now if all that is more external, more mechanical, in a man, begins to obey what is more internal in him, the internal begins to develop control of the outer or *man-machine* and the result is that the order of things begins to be *reversed*. The man is no longer so easily driven by life, by external influences, by changing circumstances, and by characteristic reactions of his personality to life and by the habits of his body. He is no longer driven from outside so completely, he is no longer a slave of his body, but begins to be controlled from within, for a brief moment.

Now if you will take this idea as simply as possible, you will see to some extent that the possession of a *Second Body* means that a man is different from an ordinary man. He is different because an ordinary man – a man-machine – is a function of life. A man-machine is driven by life, and so always acted upon by and obedient to life. That is, he is driven from outside and from the more external parts of him. But a man who has begun to have something internally organized in him is no longer so easily driven by outer life but is at times controlled from something within himself. That is, at times *he works in a reverse direction*. We may all imagine that we work already in this reverse direction, but this is only imagination. A very little sincere self-observation will show us that we are truly functions of life. We are driven by life and circumstances and have nothing or very little that is strong enough to resist being driven in this way. You must realize that each man is, of course, driven by life in a different way from other men. But all ordinary men, all men belonging to the circle of mechanical humanity ... are driven *from outside*, even though they believe that they are not. In this sense, they are *man-machines*. And this is because nothing internal in them has been developed to such an extent that they obey this internal thing and so resist the kaleidoscope of changing life. Nothing *in them* is strong enough to resist life – that is, strong enough to resist the reactions they ordinarily have to life. They certainly may notice they do not react to life as others do, and then they imagine they can resist life. This is mere illusion. Everyone reacts differently, in his or her own way. Where one person reacts, another may not. But it is all the same. It is all *mechanical* and life controls them through their particular special mechanical and habitual reactions to it. A good man fancies he is different from a bad man, an optimistic man feels he is different from a pessimistic man, a careful man thinks he is different from a careless man, and so on. Yet all are *mechanical*. All are driven by life. All cannot help being what they are. And if they try to be different they will all find the same difficulties of changing themselves confronting them. And this means that all are, psychologically speaking, without anything *organized in them* to resist the particular effects that life has upon them. That is, they all work, or rather, are worked, from the life-side. They are all different kinds of machines, reacting or working in different ways, but all are driven by the impact of outer life. They are mechanically good, mechanically bad, mechanically optimistic, mechanically pessimistic, mechanically this and mechanically that. That is the teaching of the Work about Mechanicalness – about undeveloped Man, the *Man-Machine*, who serves Nature. But the Work teaches that Man can cease to be a machine by an inner development of individuality, consciousness and will – that is, of precisely those qualities that mechanical man imagines he already possesses. In a fully-developed man – that is, a man possessing individuality, consciousness and will – it is not life and changing outer circumstances that mechanically drive him. Such a man has something *organized* in him which can resist life, something from which he can act. Such a man, in short, *can do*. And this is because he possesses more bodies than the one he received at birth.

The Work speaks almost from its starting-point of the Essence in Man being undeveloped. It defines a growth of Essence as a change in the level of Being: and it speaks very often about making Personality passive so that Essence can develop. Especially does it speak of False Personality or Imaginary "I" and the necessity of observing ourselves in regard to these and separating from them. The object of this is to allow something else to grow. Essence can develop. It is where a man can grow from. And in connection with the development of Essence a second body can grow. But it cannot do so as long as Personality is active and controls the inner life. . . . *Personality is active and Essence is passive* in mechanical man and this is due to the action of Life that keeps this relationship between Personality and Essence. Life is the neutralizing force that keeps Personality active and Essence passive.

There is only one force that can change this relationship of Personality and Essence – a force coming from *outside life*. This is the Work, or, in general, *conscious influences*, coming from the Conscious Circle of Humanity, outside mechanical life. . . . For the Work, coming from Conscious Influences, can form in suitable soil, a receptive organ through which a man can receive force – that is, his "daily bread." And since Essence is the most real part of a man and Personality *relatively* unreal, for this organ to form itself aright, it must eventually form itself out of what is *most real and sincere* in a man. It cannot form itself in the external man, nor in the hypocrite in a man which is the False Personality. . . .

It (the Work) says that Personality must be properly formed first of all, and, unless it is, Essence cannot grow beyond a limited point. Essence grows a little and then Personality must form round it. Then Essence *can* grow by using the food of Personality, that is, by making Personality passive. So you see that Man, properly understood, is a series of experiments on himself. A badly formed Personality, in conjunction with a childish Essence, handicaps a man. The idea is that a man must go *out* of himself into life, and, as it were, come back again – a movement similar to that of the prodigal son. Life must act on a man fully before Essence can grow beyond its natural point . . . it can grow to a certain point where it is still childish. . . . And then it stops. Personality must now form the potential, eventual food for Essence and so Personality must be formed and become active. A man must learn all about the life he is born into on this earth. Later, if he has magnetic center, and if he wishes, he may find the means of making his developed Personality passive by long inner work. By doing so, he feeds Essence through inner struggle.

Now the formation of second body is connected with a growth of Essence, which is internal to Personality. . . . Essence must be *taught* to develop. The Work does not start from Essence. It starts, in a man having magnetic center, from those "I's" in him which wish to work, and they form "Deputy-Steward." This is the first point of Work made in a man. It can break up: or it can become stronger. These "I's" must *teach Essence* – that is, Personality must, at first, teach Essence. . . . Deputy-Steward must then struggle not only with wrong or ignorant "I's" in Personality, with wrong mental and emotional habits, with False Personality, with sleep, with imagination, with internal considering, with identifying, with lying, with negative emotions, with self-justifying, and so on, but also with undeveloped or childish Essence. For the evolution of the man himself depends on a development of his Essence:

and a development of his Essence is connected with the formation in him of "second body."

We have already made a few approaches to the idea of further bodies in Man than the physical body. This lecture on the Four Bodies, given many years ago by G and recorded by Mr. Ouspensky, must be taken as a general survey.

"According to an ancient teaching, traces of which may be found in many systems, old and new, a man who has attained the full development possible for Man, a man in the full sense of the Word, *consists of Four bodies*. These four bodies are composed of substances which are finer and finer, mutually interpenetrate one another and form four independent organisms, standing in a definite relationship to one another but capable of independent action.

"The reason why it is possible for four bodies to exist is that the human organism, that is, the physical body, has such complex organization that, under certain conditions, a new independent organism can grow in it, affording a much more convenient and responsive instrument for the activity of consciousness than the physical body. The consciousness manifested in this new body is capable of governing and having full power and control over the physical body. In this second body, under certain conditions, a third body can grow, again having characteristics of its own. The consciousness manifested in this third body has full power and control over the first two bodies; and the third body possesses the possibility of acquiring knowledge inaccessible either to the first or to the second body. In the third body, under certain conditions, a fourth can grow, which differs as much from the third as the third differs from the second and the second from the first. The consciousness manifested in the fourth body has full control over the first three bodies and itself.

"These four bodies are defined in different teachings in various ways.... The first is the physical body, in Christian terminology the 'carnal' body; the second, in Christian terminology, is the 'natural' body; the third is the 'spiritual' body; and the fourth, in the terminology of *esoteric Christianity*, is the 'divine' body.

"In the terminology of certain Eastern teachings the first body is the *carriage* (body), the second body is the *horse* (feelings, desires), the third, the *driver* (mind) and the fourth, the *master* ('I', consciousness, will).

"Such comparisons and parallels may be found in most systems and teachings which recognize something more in Man than the physical body. But almost all these teachings, while repeating in a more or less familiar form the definitions and divisions of the ancient teaching, have forgotten or omitted its most important feature which is that Man is not born with the finer bodies, and that they can only be artificially cultivated in him provided favorable conditions, both internal and external, are present.

"The 'second body' is not an indispensable implement for Man. A man can live quite well without a second body. His physical body possesses all the functions necessary for life.

"This applies still more, of course, to the 'third body' and the 'fourth body.' Ordinary man does not possess those bodies or their corresponding functions. The reasons for this are, first, the fact that the physical body works with the same substances of which the higher bodies are composed, only these substances are not crystallized in him, and so do not belong to him; and secondly, it has all the functions analogous to those of the higher bodies, though of course they differ from them considerably. The chief difference between a man possessing the physical body and the other functions undeveloped, and a man possessing the developed functions of all four bodies, is that, in the first case, the *physical body* governs all the other functions – in other words, everything is governed by the body which, in its turn, is governed by the external influences of life:

such a man is governed by life. In the second case, the command or control emanates from the higher bodies and so a man is no longer governed by outer life.

"... In relation to the undeveloped functions of a man of physical body only, the automaton or man-machine depends upon external influences, and the next three functions depend upon the physical body and the external influences it receives. Changing desires and aversions – 'I want,' 'I don't want,' 'I like,' 'I don't like' – that is, functions occupying the place of the second body, depend upon accidental shocks and influences. Thinking, which corresponds to the functions of the third body, is an entirely mechanical process. 'Will' is absent in ordinary mechanical man – he has desires only; and a greater or lesser *permanence* of desires and wishes is called a strong or a weak will.

"In the second case – that is, in relation to the developed functions of the four bodies – the working of the physical body depends upon the influences of the other or higher bodies. Instead of the discordant and often contradictory activity of different desires, there is *one single 'I'*, whole, indivisible and permanent; there is *individuality*, dominating the physical body and its desires, and able to overcome both its reluctance and its resistance. Instead of the mechanical process of thinking there is *consciousness*. And there is *will* – that is, a power, not merely composed of various, often contradictory, desires belonging to different "I's", but issuing from consciousness and governed by individuality or a single and permanent 'I.' Only such a will can be called 'free,' for it is independent of accident and cannot be altered or directed from without.

"An Eastern teaching describes the function of the four bodies, their gradual growth and the conditions of this growth, in the following way:

"Let us imagine a vessel or a retort filled with various metallic powders. The powders are not in any way connected with each other and every accidental change in the position of the retort or vessel, every accidental knock it receives, changes the relative position of the loose powders. If the retort be shaken or tapped with the finger, then the powder which was at the top may appear at the bottom or in the middle, while the one which was at the bottom may appear at the top. There is nothing permanent in the position of the powders and under such conditions there can be nothing permanent. This is an exact picture of our psychic life, which changes at every moment. Each succeeding moment new influences may change the position of the powder which is on the top and put in its place another which is absolutely its opposite. Science calls this state of the powders the state of mechanical mixture. The essential characteristic of the interrelation of the powders to one another in this kind of mixture is the instability of these interrelations and their variability.

"It is impossible to stabilize the interrelation of powders in a state of merely mechanical mixture. But the powders may be *fused;* the nature of the powders makes this possible. To do this a special kind of fire must be lighted under the retort which, by heating and melting the powders, finally fuses them together. Fused in this way the powders will be no longer a mechanical mixture but in a state of chemical union. And now they can no longer be separated by those simple methods which separated them and made them change places when they were in a state of mechanical mixture. The contents of the retort have become indivisible, 'individual,' by fusion. This is a picture of the formation of the second body. The fire by means of which fusion is attained is produced by friction, which, in its turn, is produced in a man by the struggle between 'yes' and 'no' within him. If a man gives way to himself at all times, if he gives way to all his desires and moods, to his changing thoughts, there will be no inner struggle in him, no friction, and so *no fire*. But if, for the sake of attaining a definite aim, he struggles with himself, if he struggles with the thoughts and desires that hinder him, he will then create a fire which will gradually transform his inner world into a single whole.

"Let us return to our example. The chemical compound obtained by fusion of the powders in the retort possesses certain qualities, comparable to a certain specific gravity, a certain electrical conductivity and so on. These qualities constitute the characteristics of the substance in question. But by means of work upon it of a certain kind the number of these characteristics may be increased, that is, the fused alloy may be given new properties which did not primarily belong to it. It may be possible to create inner changes in it, to make it radioactive, and so on.

"The process of imparting new properties to the fused alloy corresponds to the process of the formation of the third body and of the acquisition of new knowledge and powers with the help of the third body.

"When the third body has been formed and has acquired all the properties, powers and knowledge possible for it, there remains the problem of fixing and directing this knowledge and these powers, because, having been imparted to it by influences of a certain kind, they may be taken away by these same influences or by others. By means of a special kind of work the acquired properties may be made the permanent and inalienable possession of the third body. The process of fixing these acquired properties corresponds to the process of the formation of the fourth body, through which the 'Master' works.

"Only the man who possesses four fully-developed bodies can be called a 'man' in the full sense of the word. This man possesses very many properties which ordinary man does not possess and *one of these properties is immortality*. All religions and all ancient teachings contain the idea that, by acquiring the fourth or divine body Man acquires immortality; and they all contain indications of the ways to acquire the fourth body – that is, immortality.

"In this connection certain teachings compare Man with a house of four rooms. Man lives in one room, the smallest and the poorest of all, and, until he is told of it, he does not suspect the existence of the other rooms which are full of treasures. When he does learn of this he begins to seek the keys of these rooms and especially of the fourth, the most important room of all. And when a man has found his way into this room he really becomes the master of his house, for only then does the house belong to him, wholly and for ever.

"The fourth room gives Man true immortality and all religious teachings strive to show the way to it. There are a great many ways, some shorter, some longer, some harder and some easier, but all, without exception, lead or strive to lead, in one direction, that is, to immortality."

MARY C. FULLERSON

Discovery of Intimate Order

At twelve years it was said of him in whom the Christ would come to dwell: "Jesus increased in wisdom and stature and in favor with God and man." And of himself at twelve, he said, "I must be about my Father's business."

Here is a model of serene and exquisite order, the balanced order of evolving body and mind, of committed will, of righteousness towards brother, of upward thrust towards God.

Here is wholeness; all is proper for persuasion; all is well. The bodies of being move in symmetry to reach the petalled opening of awareness as a single form.

Ideally, the inner world of every man is thus designed for orbed and holy order and only waits for him to recognize the call at core of being. The process of becoming should move in sequence and precision as soon as there is conscious will-to-evolve.

But it is unlikely to be as straightforward as this today. However single-eyed may be the resolve for disciplined self-development, we are distracted by Nature's erratic course and the threat of madness in men; while beyond the sense of helplessness which these cast, we bear unprecedented physical-psychological restlessness, for our bodies are becoming radioactive, cell by cell.

Disruption and distress without . . . confusion and bewilderment within . . . and a new urgency for central peace. This is the mood we meet in almost every mind, for the concern is world-size now. When pictures of the Earth were made from space, one caught one's breath in awful recognition of the single sweep of destiny earth holds, and no man's age or color or location or belief exempts him from the need to face the same demand.

A first reaction is usually desire to run to whatever place or precept appears to offer cloister, and indeed monasticism was the way persons and treasures of an earlier time were saved. But the dangers are different now, and if we try to repeat the solution in literal terms we fail, for there is no longer a geographical or purely ideological refuge anywhere.

Yet there must be prescience in the urge for flight, and wisdom in wanting to draw protection from a quality of thought. From pivotal problem, pivotal promise comes; and almost certainly there will be a new monasticism as men grow in knowledge of Essence and learn to make obeisance at the inner altar of evolving truth.

Of this I presume to speak. As one pressed to seek, I speak of what I've found. If hereafter the pronoun "we" is often used, it is because of the discovery of how little one finds alone.

We are not likely to outreach the need to regard the adage: "Know thyself," – least of all now. Now of all times, we need to be seeing true. When almost every outer thing we thought was stable is trembling on the ground of change, we need essential, inner certainties. We need to know who we are, where we are in space and time, and what is our intimate size – and then, for sake of poise, to carry this orientation in steady thoughtfulness.

To misjudge identity, or miscalculate size, tilts the subconscious scales, while not to be sure of place can only deepen wonder if there be a wall . . .

Who are we?
      Where are we?
           What is our size?

The call is to see *true* – to look back as far as the beginning of the sentient soul. Cloaks of embodiment have come and gone in useful sequence, but the permanent "I" holds continuity. I-was; I-am; I-am-to-be in time and purpose, and the present life is only a segment of the ongoing whole.

The precocious and the wise have known how to look upon the wide screen of existence in this way, although on earlier rounds many of us may still have taken a shuttered view. But now we need to sight straight across the full phenomenon of rebirth and acknowledge it as the way to reckon subjective size.

History is diminished if read as if it gave account of ancient peoples in unrelated times, forgetting the I-was-there of our own past tense, or that it tells the past of other men living today.

We are as large as every life we have had, and yet as small as each must be in the vast aggregate of successive lives of all mankind and the evolving majesty of Earth and stars.

This is the kind of measurement we must accommodate if we are to resist the incredible pressure upon the basic structure of personal entity.

And where are we now?

It follows that on the revolving stage of circumstance we are where we should be to experience conditions not experienced or not dealt with fully on the previous course. By pre-birth choice or pre-birth requirement we have come, and the soul's serene prevision was satisfied by the terms of its re-entry or we would not be here!

We are where we are by having been, as well as by being now. With creative imagination we can move through time to see beginning and ongoing for ourselves and others and discover spatial brotherhood. Illusions of psychic distance fall away, and the sense-of-place emerges as the path of one's progression as a soul among the progressing souls of all humanity.

We are all seasoned travelers and should be able to take the sophisticated traveler's attitude towards others along the way, for assuredly each can say: "I have been or shall be of both high and low degree; I have been weak and strong, gifted and stupid, born with each gender, and had several kinds of skins . . . .

"And I have probably sat at the feet of most of the great Masters or been taught by those who did. Surely the distilled accomplishment of the moral-ethical strains of personal "East" and "West" can meet the compass points of other men without occasion for emotional conflict or petty argument . . .

"Only if I've forgot my own intimate record can I walk on the opposite side of a road I once have walked and not salute the man who has changed places with me there . . .

"Only if I've forgotten the feeling of a different skin stretched upon the frame of enduring essence can I turn from one that I once wore or will be wearing in time. . . ."

Lack of tolerance is lack of memory, but the effect is bewilderment in what seems to be a mapless world of lost relationships. True bearing comes by way of purposeful, dispassionate recall.

Then, who are we?

On the grand scale of ultimate Order, at no less than the voicing of "LET!" we ask for an answer to this. For man had to be free to turn from primary Order and thus learn its necessity; and in life after life after life there has been the tension of soul between impulse towards wholeness and impulse towards forfeiture; while through the recurring cycles, an ego-of-person was forming that could lead to self-recognition and return to centrality.

In the magnificent plan for such a vast learning event, Masters of Wisdom were allowed to reveal the manifold aspects of truth They discerned as Interpreters. We have the sacred accrual to serve as continuing strength.

The great epochs of growth have dawned ... developed ... declined.... When it is time for the next, the pulse of Earth quickens to accept an astonishing thrust. On the eve of new revelation, the Teachers acknowledge advance, for They – as those They have taught – are progressing towards further truth.

But at the first stir of change, man's ego may suddenly falter, forgetting its earned intent, and try to recover the semblance of what was known to be good, but is now no longer enough – to return to what has been mastered, a rest it cannot afford.

Then persuasions that foster the sleep of non-response have appeal, and any irregular means of stepping past normal consciousness become the sirens that call....

This is the critical factor in times of large scale transitions: that fearing to meet what is new, the ego may attempt abdication for sake of a phantom of peace; or that thinking itself to be helpless before the size of demand, may try to find psychic enlargement for sake of false adequacy.

But whether denied or depressed or strained by unnatural increase, the ego remains – the personal presence-of-being, though burdened, unbalanced, distraught. Too much is at stake not to see the necessity here. The question: Who are we? is almost a desperate one.

Who are we? Who are we, indeed?

We are the inviolate Essence of the enduring wonder of life – continuing ego and spirit traversing the ages of breath ... long, long prepared to be able to answer to promise of power.... No kind of appraisal suffices to evidence worth of this sort ... value, incredible value – made in the Image of God – offered the role of co-builder in the orderly process of growth....

We are abiding Earth-dwellers, allotted the trust of her care ... the regenerative agents appointed to see her distress and restore her to habits of health. No demand for redemption but is matched by capacity, when – as workers-of-change – we accept the noble commitment to nurture the seeds of tomorrow.

And yet of ourselves we are nothing! The paradox baffles the heart. We are the heirs of Creation ... yet, of ourselves, nothing at all....

At the point of exquisite balance between the poles of this truth, rests the intimate order of being the soul is designed to require....

And here is the New Revelation – here stands the Etheric Christ – not as Teacher, or Prophet, or Leader, but as palpable Presence – LIFE! ... Life that transmutes radiation by fact of Its Radiance ... peace beyond understanding, even in physical cells ... retreat from confusion of heart without leaving the seething world ... cloistered the Realization:

Not I
    but
        Christ-*in*-me....

Order, intimate Order – comes of Christ Chemistry.

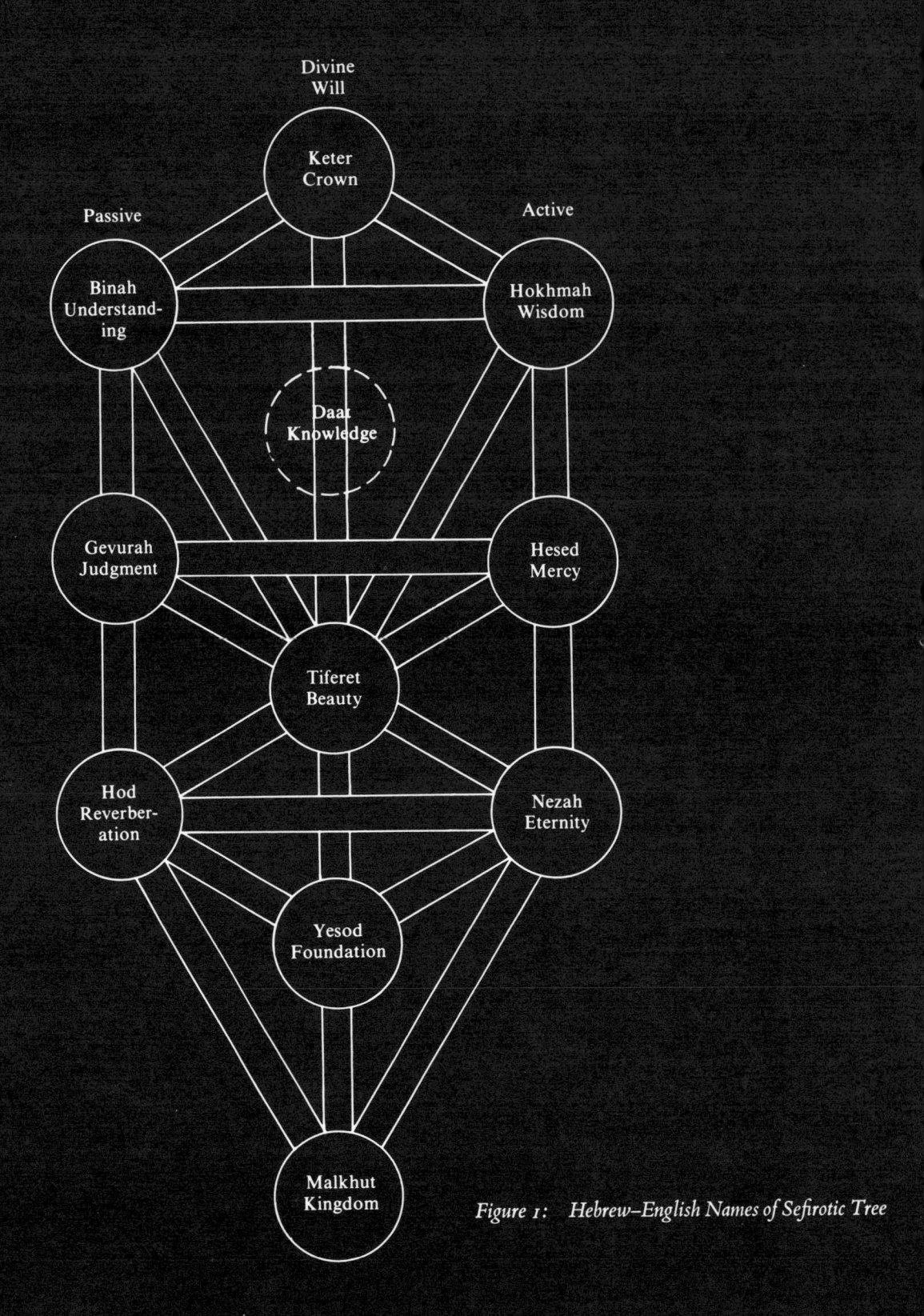

Figure 1: Hebrew–English Names of Sefirotic Tree

Z'EV BEN SHIMON HALEVI
Order: A Kabbalistic Approach

KABBALAH is the name for a body of objective knowledge. Its origin is the inner Teaching of Judaism. Its concern is the nature of God, the Universe and man, and their mutual interrelation. Tradition states that it was given by God to the higher Archangels who passed it on to man, and thus a chain of instruction has been maintained throughout the hierarchy of Worlds that comprise existence. Historically speaking, the first Kabbalist in the Judaic line was Abraham, who was initiated by Melchezedek. From him, the Knowledge was passed down over the generations through the patriarchs to Moses, who transmitted it to Joshua and the Elders. From late Biblical times, it was taught by those who received it via tradition or revelation, that is, the line of priests and prophets. Changing its outer form and name from period to period, the Teaching continually stated the essential instruction about the Total Reality of Existence. By the Middle Ages, this inner Torah came to be called Kabbalah, or "What has been received." Cast in a mixture of Rabbinical and scholastic terminology it has come down to us today when it yet again is being restated in contemporary terms, so that this generation may comprehend the purpose of Existence. What follows is a very brief account of the theory and practice of the Kabbalistic system of Order.

Before the beginning of anything there was only God. Nothing existed, not even Existence. Tradition states that God, being Nothing and All, therefore wished to see God, that is God's reflection or image, and so God willed Existence into Existence. This was accomplished, it is allegorically explained, by God withdrawing from a portion of Totality, thus allowing for a space wherein Existence could become. Into this space, we are told, the Will of God projected a line of light which unfolded according to God's Mercy and Justice as well as God's Will. These three aspects of Divinity, by their interaction, precipitated a sequence of events in which Divinity manifested in Ten perfect and unchanging Attributes. As such these Ten Utterances, or lights, or vessels (they have many traditional names), composed an archetypal World in which God was reflected. The total image contained is sometimes called Adam Kadmon, the primordial man, or simply the Glory of God. Upon this perfect model, all subsequent Worlds, entities and organizations were to be based.

The most well known exposition of the Divine World of Emanation, as this first level of Existence came to be called, is the Sefirotic Tree of Life. There are others just as detailed, but none so graphically clear. Basically the "Tree" is composed of Ten principles or sefirot plus one non-sefirah. These are based upon the interaction of the Divine laws of Will, Mercy and Justice and the sequence of stages needed to make Existence stable yet flexible. Thus, a system beginning with the Crown at the top of the Tree emanates out of the One, through the duality of active and passive complements, to a supernal trinity that is repeated downwards in three triads, before resolving in the final sefirah of Malkhut, the Kingdom, at the bottom of the Tree. As a result of this interaction of triads there is set up a complex of relationships which subdivide into active, passive and equalizing triads. These again break down into paths which relate one sefirah to another. As will be noted, it rapidly becomes a very subtle scheme

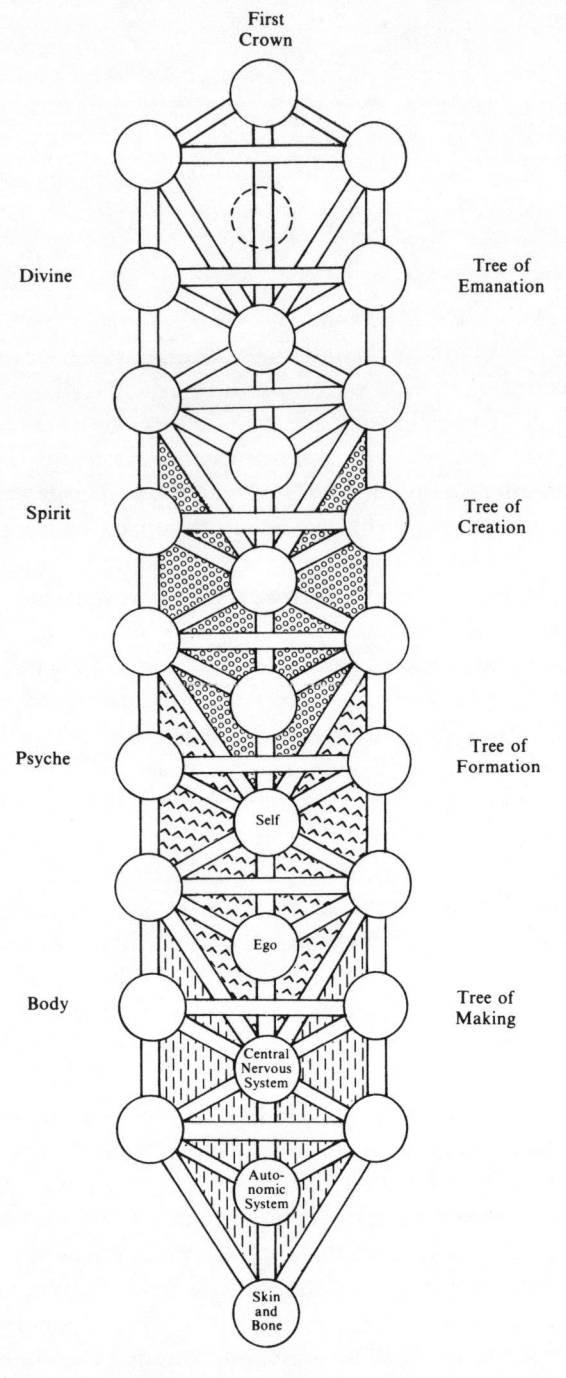

Figure 2: The Four Worlds

of checks and balances, levels and flows. However, for our purpose it is only necessary to know the general design and function.

Broadly speaking, there is the principle of Unity, in that the whole Tree is in fact a Divine Singleness; that there is the active and passive aspect of perfection as expressed in the side pillars, and that besides the triad principle, which is engendered by the above, there is also a four-layered sequence within the Ten-stage unfolding of the sefirot (plural of sefirah).

Out of the four layers generated by the other laws came what were to be known as the three lower separated Worlds. These removes from perfect unity are called Creation, Formation and Making. The World of Creation, it is said, emerges out of the second layer of Emanation to unfold as a complete Tree in its own right with all the sefirotic laws present but at a lesser potency. Indeed, this could not be otherwise because of the separation from the Divine World of Emanations; and so out of the Time-fullness of the Eternal Unchanging emerges time and its consequent effects. Here begins the Cosmic manifestation of the Universe. It is called in Kabbalah the World of Pure Spirit or Heaven.

Out of the midst of Creation issues the World of Formation. This is the echo of the third level of Emanation and here again a complete Tree emerges with its own sefirotic complement. Being yet another remove from the Divine World, it is less potent than the World of Creation. Moreover, its nature is as different as Creation is to Emanation. It is the realm of everchanging forms and corresponds, in human terms, to the level of the soul or psyche. The fourth World, that of Making or Action, emerges out of that of Formation and brings into existence the physical world of Nature and the elements that comprise the sensually perceived Universe. There is a fifth World below. This is schematically Hell or the cosmic cesspool where the refuse of Existence is stored and reprocessed before re-use.

From the foregoing it will be seen that Kabbalists perceive Existence as a ladder of interpenetrating Worlds, each of which is based on the Divine sefirotic model of the first image of Adam Kadmon. From this notion it is possible, Kabbalists say, to examine the physical, psychological and spiritual organization of a human being, because man, like the original Adam, is made in the image of his maker. This premise is based on the fact that the Divine laws that operate above also occur below, though of course in a denser materiality and more sluggish energy range. This coarser phenomenon is the result of the multiplication of laws as Existence becomes more complicated with the descent of the Creative impulse. The exact reverse is true in the evolutionary impulse of Teshuvah, or return, wherein a human being rises back up to the Divine presence again. This latter process is the work of Kabbalah. However, before we can speak of practice, there must be the preparation of theory, because in the Way of Kabbalah every step of the return sequence must be completed. Let us begin by briefly examining the human physical body.

Conforming to the first sefirotic principle, the body is a unity as an organism. Likewise in accord with the second Law, that is the passive and active principle, the body manifests as matter and energy. The third Law or the Trinity is completed by the presence of will that makes it conscious. The organization of the body, moreover, divides into the four-layer levels of a Tree, in that it contains a physical, chemical, electronic and conscious level of operation. Here, the conscious level would correspond to the Divine aspect of the organism. On the form side pillar are to be found the frame, anabolic and harmonizing sefirot that support, build and monitor the body, while on the active pillar are to be discovered the activating life principle, the energy release and physical input processes. On the central column are to be located the bone and skin at Malkhut, the autonomic Foundation of Yesod and the central nervous system at Tiferet, traditionally called the Seat of Solomon because of its junctional position. Above is the Daat or Knowledge of the body which acts as the connection with the World of the psyche above. The Crown of the Tree is the simultaneous Tiferet of the psychological World and the Malkhut of the Tree of the Spirit. This is the Source of the body.

The minor triads of the physical Tree are concerned either with active or passive processes of the muscles and nerves, organs, cells, metabolism and electro-magnetic organism, or the degrees of mineral, vegetable and animal consciousness within the body. This leads on to the first step in Kabbalistic practical work of recognizing different areas of operation in the body and lower psyche.

The preliminary stages of practice after the theory of the sefirotic Tree has been learnt is to realize the natural basis of our existence. In this one has to study and separate the mineral tendencies to be inert or continually to move, according to the influences from outside. Included in the examination of the mineral aspects of ourselves is the observation of elemental states of solid, liquid, gaseous and radiant conditions in which we are stable or rigid, flexible or flaccid, energetic or frenetic, illuminated or blasted. In a similar way the Kabbalist has to note his inherent vegetable nature in that he eats, drinks, excretes, grows, procreates, grows old, decays and dies. Included in his vegetable studies are the response to pleasant and unpleasant phenomena, fertile and barren conditions, and monthly and annual cycles of vitality. During the course of this examination, the student begins to separate out the mineral and vegetable levels of his daily life, so exposing the animal aspects of his Nefesh or Vital Soul which enjoys company, must compete, dominate, move, satisfy its curiosity, and generally live within a social order. This animal aspect is quite different from the vegetable, because whereas the plants desire only to survive in greatest comfort, the animal soul will risk experiment and even sacrifice its life for the herd or tribe. Along with this animal phenomenon are all the attributes of cunning, skill in hunt and evasion, friendship, animosity, jealousy, passion, devotion, amusement and gamesmanship which people consider as human qualities. In fact, they are the strictly animal part of mankind. With the animal soul comes simple intelligence, memory, invention, imagination and the capacity to dream. All this level of experience has to be taken into account and deducted from the Kabbalist's life experience in order to arrive at what is truly human, which for most of us at this stage is not much, despite our ego overlay of education and opinion. Here begins the study of the World of the psyche, which is the natural habitat of the human race.

Kabbalistic tradition states that mankind fell from Eden or the World of Formation and was given coats of skin. That is, in Biblical terms, the psyche, represented by Adam and Eve, was incarnated into flesh or a natural body composed of mineral, vegetable and animal levels of matter, energy and consciousness. Thus, a human being is half immersed in the World of Nature, with the upper part of his psyche hidden out of range of the natural mind in the upper half of the Tree of Formation or the Unconscious. This is the situation a person finds him or herself in recognizing that they do not wish to live like a stone, a plant or an animal, that is free from the dominance of Nature, who only seeks to make one part of a mass, never an individual. Thus, the second step in Kabbalah is to separate the human part of oneself from the Nefesh or Vital Soul, not by denying it but by dealing intelligently with it so that it makes minimal demands. In this state of physical equilibrium, the work on the psyche can begin.

The lower part of the psychological Tree fits over the upper part of the physical Tree with the Malkhut of Formation, or the base connection of the psyche, superimposed on the Tiferet or central nervous system of the body, where brain tissue and lower psyche interpenetrate. Above, over the Daat or Knowledge of the body lies the Yesod, or Foundation, of the psyche. This is the ordinary ego-mind that deals with external matters and screens the imagery of the interior events of the psyche. While the Malkhut of the psyche can be said to contain all the genetic factors of a person's psyche, that is, his family and nation and all its inherited characteristics, the Foundation or ego is of a different order. This Yesod of the psyche is the place where the culture and manners are imbibed. It is that part of us that can be influenced and educated to be sophisticated or bigoted, tolerant or puritanical. In short, it is that part of us that is most open or closed to immediate change. Normally in social situations, this ego wears a mask or persona that is acceptable not only to others but to ourselves, because that is how we imagine we really are. This, it is soon discovered, is not so when the Self, that hovers just above the ego on the psychological Tree, is seen to be the essence of a person. However, before this stage is reached, it is necessary to observe the composition of the ego.

It will be noted that the ego is at the center of a great triangle which, again, is made up of three sub-triads. The great triangle is the field of mental mechanics. That is the workaday mechanism, the autonomic mechanisms of thinking, feeling, and action. Here, the interior and exterior events of a person's life are dealt with in one of three ways. Depending on the temperament, one of the processes will dominate so that one person will be considered a thinker, another a feeler, and another a doer. In Kabbalah one of the first psychological exercises is to recognise one's own psycho-body type and to cultivate the other two triads in order to balance the ego. This is done by work on theory and practice. For example, the thinker may be given practical problems to solve, while the doer is made to write poetry, and the

Figure 3: Body-Psyche

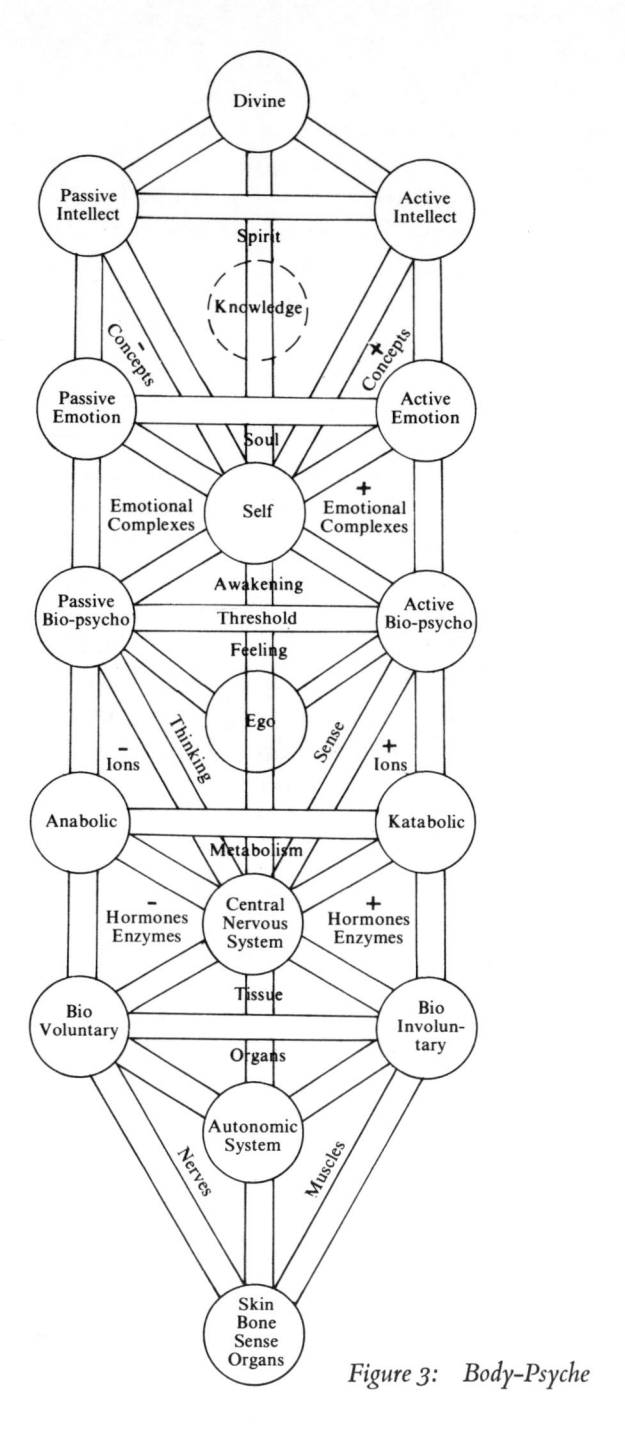

feeler learns some intellectual skill. This process also teaches the ego to become obedient and discard many of its habitual patterns. Often the process is long, and sometimes the student will continually retreat from a real committment to Kabbalistic work. This crisis is often brought to a head by the phenomenon that the person begins to undergo change, so that sometimes he, and particularly his old cronies, no longer recognize his personality. The frequent solution is that his habitual friends soon ignore this "new man" who no longer plays their games, while he learns to readjust to a different way of working in life and forms new relationships.

The transformation of the ego is the first major step in Kabbalistic work, because while a person may study the subject assiduously, until he begins to actually change, it remains merely an academic operation, no matter how much he may work at theory and practice. To change means growth, and this requires the death of the old personality and its useless patterns. Because there are few who are prepared to do this, Kabbalah is only for those who are willing to sacrifice and risk their psychological or social wealth. This does not necessarily mean to sell all that you have, but as one great Kabbalist put it, to be prepared to. The shock of giving up one's personal fantasies about oneself, for example, is often more than most people's ego can stand. That is why Kabbalah is traditionally only recommended to the mature who have ridden out the storms of vicissitude in life and come through in strength and stability. Kabbalah promises no easy or quick method of enlightenment. It is a slow but sound progression up Jacob's ladder.

The next step is to cross the threshold between the Hod and Nezah of the psyche. These two sefirot are the active and passive aspects of the bio-psycho organism. Half in the body and half in the psyche, they function as the communication and repeating principles in the body-mind. Thus the active side holds the circuits of memory, for instance, while the passive responds and connects the memories, as both file their input onto the mind-brain screen of the psychological Yesod of the ego consciousness. As may be observed, this creates a highly complex system which gives the ego a kaleidoscopic or chameleon-like nature. It is not without reason that Yesod is given the patriarchal image of Joseph of the coat of many colors. However, with the crossing of the threshold between Hod and Nezah the beginning of the conscious unification of the psyche begins.

The threshold, in modern psychological terms, is the frontier of the unconscious. Beyond this line lies, for most people, a hidden depth from which emotions and thoughts emerge. By this is meant not just feelings or mental routines but real emotion and intellect. Most moods, for example, belong to the lower part of the psyche and are in fact generated by the body. Real emotions and thoughts occur deep in the psyche and are present rather like the unseen stars in the daytime of ordinary ego consciousness. With the crossing of the threshold and the coming into the awareness of the Self, an awakened state is precipitated. This heightened condition is known to everyone through the experience of love, or a moment of deep stillness or great awe. It is not uncommon, but what is unusual is for it to be obtained by will. This the Kabbalist seeks to do. Will is a crucial tool in Kabbalistic work.

There are many kinds of will. First there is the will of the body which demands its comforts and satisfactions. Then there is the will of the ego which requires its importance being acknowledged. This it accomplishes by willfulness or will-lessness, depending on whether the active or passive side of the ego is predominant. For the Kabbalist the next step in training is to get the ego to be willing. This difficult task having been accomplished, the following phase is to develop the skill to be able to cross the threshold by self-volition and so enter into the triad of awakened consciousness by choice rather than chance. The lucid condition of awakened consciousness is called Gadlut in Kabbalah which means the greater as against the lesser, Katnut, or ordinary state.

The above achievement is obtained by the development of "my will." The term "my will" is generated by the ability to operate not from ego, but from the self which is situated at the center of the psychological Tree. The self is that part of us that only gradually changes over a lifetime. While the body may bloom and wither and the ego undergo all sorts of transformations according to good or ill fortune or work on it by ourselves or others, the self remains more or less the same. Indeed so much so that we may recognise someone we were at school with many decades ago, despite their wrinkled faces and changed attitudes and demeanor. The self is that which is truly ours, our own individuality, even if it is but a facet of the Unity of Existence. It is from this place, the psychological Seat of Solomon, that our self will is made. This will is very powerful, and many people not in spiritual work know its capacity and use its power to rule and dominate lesser-willed beings. Politics, commerce, the arts and sciences are full of such individuals. Their hallmark is that they are individuals. Most people, despite their belief in their individuality, are no more than egocentric, which means they are in fact subject to external pressure, from their neighbours or from what their social-tribe and custom think they should do. The individual goes his own way.

As will be seen, to be an individual does not always mean one is good or bad. Nor does it mean one is even spiritual. This is because the place of the Self occupies the position where three sefirot meet on Jacob's Ladder. Thus it is seen that present in the self are the Keter or Crown of the body, the Teferet of the psyche, and the Malkhut of the spirit. So it is that a self can be physically dominated, psychologically orientated or spiritually committed. In the case of the Kabbalist, at this stage he is in the process of becoming psychologically acquainted with the contents of his psyche before going on to enter the bottom sefirah of the Spirit, sometimes called the Malkhut Hashamaim, or the Kingdom of Heaven. Before this stage, however, purification is required, and so the psyche's anatomy is examined and balanced.

The side sefirot of active and passive emotion and intellect make, with the two lower psycho-biological sefirot, a series of four triads. In these are stored all the emotional and intellectual complexes. Here all the emotional memories and intellectual associations are arranged in initiating or conservative stance. For example, collected round the nucleus of Hesed or Mercury a particular memory may be related to love, while another attracted to Gevurah or Judgment might be associated with fear. The same occurs with ideas taken into the psyche in youth, or even in later life, which take on a revolutionary or reactionary position. In contemporary psychology these complexes are sometimes perceived as chains, or groups, while the sefirot themselves are recognizable in archetypes. Thus the hero is the archetype of Judgment, and the trickster is seen as the psychological image of Hod, the mercurial sefirah of Reverberation, with the beautiful youth or maiden at Nezah, the sefirah of Venus. The planetary gods, of course, are simply externalizations of sefirotic principles. For the Kabbalist this interior world is not only one to be studied but to be changed.

To enter the purely psychological realm of the World of Formation requires great stability. Again this is the reason why Kabbalah requires maturity of its adherents. They must be well grounded in life and in no way rely on artificial aids such as drugs to force the pace. Indeed, tradition tells the story of four rabbis who entered the inner and upper worlds and how only one came back in good condition. So only those with patience and nerve need apply.

The process of interior observation and transformation is long and requires monitoring by someone who has been through the process himself. This guide is realized through what is called in Kabbalah a Maggid or spiritual mentor. Such a person may not necessarily be a rabbi or even Jewish. His chief qualification is that he has a contact with the Tradition. Now, there are two ways this comes about. One is through the conventional line of training in a formal school, and the other is via the oral connection of being in contact with a maggid on a one-to-one basis. The former is usually confined to rabbinical or esoteric establishments, while the latter is met usually under the most unexpected conditions. Neither connection is easy to obtain, and only persistence will gain the contact, often after many false starts and dead ends. If, however, the aspirant really desires to work in the Way of Kabbalah, providence usually provides the link in one way or another.

The function of the maggid is to both instruct and act as a channel for the influence of the upper Worlds. He is in relation to the student at the level of ego as the tempering self or will that can raise the student's level up to his own Seat of Solomon. Once the individual has reached this level and can maintain it, or at least gain it by himself, the maggid must step aside and allow the person to make his own connection with the Tradition. However, this usually only happens after many years' preparation and training.

The next phase of training, after the development of self will has been accomplished, is to learn how to give it up and convert "my will" into "Thy Will." This is the work of the triad composed by the two emotional sefirot and the self. It is called the triad of the Soul.

The Soul, it will be noted, is entirely psychological. It has no connection with the body Tree nor with the World of the Spirit, except through psychological Tiferet where it is pivoted on the Self. It is, moreover, emotional in emphasis, although it is adjacent to the intellectual concept triads. Tradition states that the soul is the garment in which the spirit is enclothed, so that one must pass through the soul when coming up from body conscious, before entering the World of the Spirit or Creation. This gives a clue to its function. The soul triad is the place where purification occurs. It is the zone of conscience, the area where good and evil contend in the psyche. Indeed, tradition says that it is here that the good and evil angels stand guard at the psychological level of Mercy and Judgment to test and tempt the soul. In modern terms this is where the psychological conflicts are worked out and resolved as the person's psyche analyzes and synthesizes the activities of the body, emotion and intellect. From a Kabbalistic view, it is the level of self-consciousness, that is awareness of the state of everything connected with one's own life and particular fate, which would include all the connections with others before birth, during life, and after death. It is here that Karma is stored or, to put it in Biblical terms, where the rewards and punishments are worked out until a third or fourth generation of that person's existence. Thus, the Kabbalist does not only work for this lifetime.

In Kabbalistic work the soul triad is also seen as the triangle of discipline, truth and love. Here, the Kabbalist meets and works with others on the Way. This is the level where a Kabbalistic group operates, each member of which acts in an active, passive, and catalytic role at some time. Thus, one person will be another's reminder in perhaps a matter of fine discrimination, while another may be the first's demonstration in forgiveness, while again someone else can be the instrument of reconciliation between two members who cannot see that they are perceiving different sides of the same psychological truth. As can be imagined, here is a very subtle form of social interaction. However, the customs and practices of such a group are unlike any ordinary social gathering where the usual animal needs of competition and display are paramount. This is a meeting where these natural elements are superseded, and the purely human values

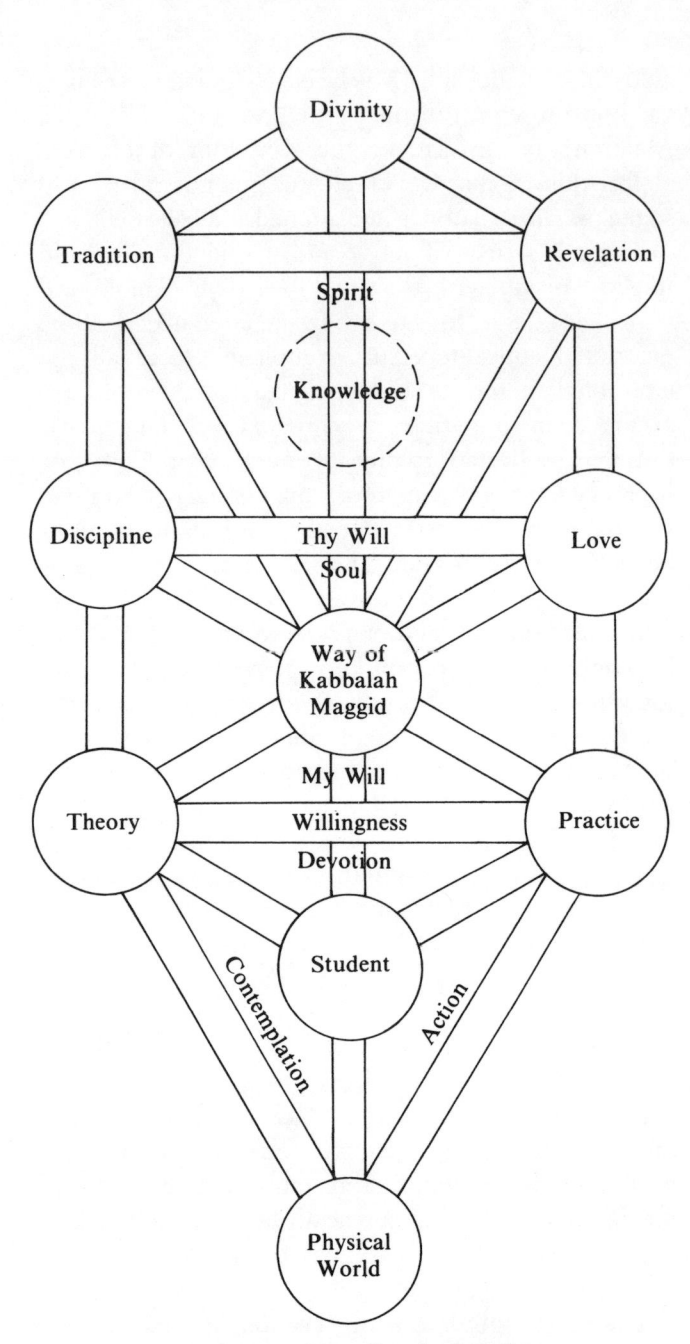

Figure 4:   Tree of Student's Path

of conscious and correct behavior in the light of spiritual aim are the criteria.

The spiritual aim of such a group is to prepare to penetrate and enter the next World. This is seen on the psychological Tree as the triad formed by the outer and inner intellectual sefirot of Binah, or Understanding, and Hokhmah, or Wisdom, and the Seat of Solomon. This great upper Triangle is, not only the deep part of the psyche, but also the overlay to the lower Face, as the kite-shaped configuration is called, of the Tree of Creation. Seen in terms of level, while the soul triad is concerned with human life and fate, the great triad of the Spirit is the psyche's direct connection with the cosmic level of human existence. Situated where it is, it acts as the focus of the Heavenly or Celestial World wherein the Destiny, or long body of a spirit's existence, is held as it passes down in the impulse of Creation, or up in the return of evolution. Here, the purpose for which that particular spirit was created is guided by the Providence that operates in the Cosmos. Thus, the lesser cycles of body and psyche are contained and controlled within the great cosmic cycle of the unfolding and refolding Universe. On this scale the individual seems insignificant, and yet he is significant, for despite the angelic monitors of this cosmic ebb and flow, the human being has free will within certain limits. This is the uniqueness of the human race, because as tradition indicates, neither the Tachutonim, those who dwell below, or the Elyonim, those who dwell above, have this privilege. The ape, however intelligent, is bound by the natural law of his species, and so too, we are told, are the angelic beings who cannot step outside their orders or celestial function. Only mankind can range throughout all the created Worlds. This gives some idea of the scale and responsibility of the World of the Spirit into which the Kabbalist seeks to enter.

At the head of the great psychological triad of the Spirit are Tradition and Revelation. From these two sefirot of Understanding and Wisdom come the influences necessary for the Kabbalist's stability between the Form and Force of Cosmic Existence. But just as important is the reception of the spiritual knowledge that comes through the Daat or unmanifest sefirah of the psyche. As will be seen, this same place is occupied by the foundation of the World of Creation, and it is on this Yesod that the Kabbalist works to build in the next stage of his ascent. Tradition states that it is from here that the purified are taught, that is those who have progressed beyond the stage of devotion at the Self. The next stage is called Sincerity, which brings the Kabbalist into the state of the Third Heaven of the seven Heavens that stretch from the self up to the Crown of Creation. The fourth state, we are told, is said "to be with God" and occupies the triad of Understanding, Wisdom and the psychological Crown. Here takes place the most esoteric of studies as the contact with the lowest sefirah of the Divine World is made.

Little has been written about this level, despite the voluminous literature of Kabbalah, because it is indescribable. There can be no image that could catch the flavor of that conjunction of psyche, spirit, and divinity. Indeed, even the greatest religious poems only retain a faint after-impression frozen in the overused medium of words. Nothing less than direct experience would satisfy the Kabbalist, and so we must be content to speculate about such a contact with Eternity.

All Traditions say that a person may go on higher and join eventually in complete unity with the Godhead, and in this, Kabbalah is no exception. However, where Kabbalah does differ from some other Ways is that it says that the Kabbalist is obligated to return to either teach what he knows or to assist in the lifting of the lower Worlds into the presence of the Divine. Thus, there are those who come down and into the Natural World by choice rather than cosmic necessity and aid those attempting to climb Jacob's Ladder. Besides this work, there is also the operation of assisting the balance of Creation, which like all creative processes undergoes stress and strain and at times is slightly off its optimum equilibrium. Such cosmic imbalances, of course, are only perceived by those whose perception is attuned to that scale of operation, that is, they are aware of the periods of excessive Form or Force that may stretch over several decades if not longer. Their lives are devoted to correcting this imbalance, and so we often find highly spiritual people in the midst of chaos like the ultra-religious Hasidim and Christians in the Nazi concentration camps. This labor is sometimes called "Work for the love of itself" and is performed by people who know the issues involved and often recognise that their lives, or deaths may be required. One does not have to look very far in history to find such people.

Kabbalah's appeal to the Western mind is particular, for despite its complexity and imagery, its methods and language are related to the Western approach, because of its practical application and Biblical mythology into which every westerner is born, be he Jew, Christian, or non-conformist. This quality makes Kabbalah the most accessible and yet the most easily misunderstood of Traditions, in that, despite its orthodox background, its name and some of its techniques and knowledge have been used for very unKabbalistic practices. While Western magic, for example, has borrowed the sefirotic Tree from Kabbalah, it must not be mistaken for the original tradition. The prime aim of Kabbalah is, not the manipulation of cosmic forces, despite the stories of Jewish folklore, but the raising of the Divine Sparks in the lower parts of Existence so that gradually the Will of God to behold God becomes realized as all the Worlds slowly cease to be separated and become one at the End of Time. It is not without reason that Kabbalah is sometimes called the Work of Unification.[1]

---

[1] For a more detailed account of this Kabbalistic approach see the author's *Tree of Life*, *Adam and Kabbalistic Tree*, *Way of Kabbalah*. All books published in London by Reder and in New York by Samuel Weiser.

KARLFRIED GRAF VON DÜRCKHEIM

On the Double Origin of Man

The Body Which We Are

OUR traditional conception of embodiment suffers from the dualistic notion of a soulless body standing in opposition to a disembodied soul and in some mysterious way connected to it.[1] With respect to *man*, as we encounter him in our everyday dealings, as we love or fear him, this division does not hold. Who has ever seen a soulless body running around, or a disembodied soul? Is a corpse still a human being?

If you ask someone to whom you are talking who he really hears, the body or the soul (in the traditional conception there is no third alternative), you will probably receive the answer: "The voice that I hear is something physical. *What* I hear is, however, something psycho-spiritual, and so I therefore hear a psycho-physical unity, or else a unity of body and soul." Such an answer is an evasion, in which it becomes clear that what is immediately given has slipped out of view. The simple answer to the question "Whom do you hear?" must surely be, simply, "I hear you!" One hears me, this particular someone, who is, as such, beyond the opposition of body and soul. If in the science of man we learned to take this someone as seriously as we do in our everyday dealings with our fellow human beings, a new chapter would begin in the history of knowledge, but also of education, therapeutic treatment, and spiritual guidance! We are today in the throes of beginning this chapter. We are starting to take man seriously as the someone, i.e. the person there in front of us in the flesh, who beyond the opposition of body and soul, or body and spirit, *is* there. But this also means a change in our conception of the body.

It is a remarkable fact that for the Far East, for whose world view "incarnation" is the basic evil, the body has played a decisive role as the medium of transcendental transparency, whereas the Christian West, for whom the Incarnation, spirit becoming flesh, holds a central position, has continually experienced and condemned the body as an adversary, a hindrance, and a distraction on the path to salvation. At best, the body has a merely secular and pragmatic significance. The body, as such, seems to be far removed from all spiritual reality. It is therefore, no wonder that ancient oriental disciplines of the body, if as in the case of Hatha Yoga, they maintain their incursion into the West, are taught and practiced primarily as a kind of physical gymnastics. When practiced in this way, their true initiatory meaning as "Union with the Absolute" is lost.

In our culture, the body is understood quite one-sidedly as an instrument with which to survive, "get on," and be productive in the world. So it is "trained" and handled like a piece of apparatus that must be kept in good condition, reliable, flexible and "well oiled," in order to function efficiently and without friction. But such "treatment" concerns only the body that one "has." Its functioning usually has, as great figures in sport prove often enough, very little to do with inner maturity or the way of initiation. Something completely different happens if, instead of training the body merely for efficiency of functioning and performance, one tries to put it in the service of inner transformation. Then, it is a question not of the body that one has, but the body that one *is*. This is a critical distinction for all personal therapy, i.e., therapy not just of the body but of the human being. And it is no less important with respect to the inner path; for just as the physical soundness of the body is not in itself sufficient for the ordinary man's adequate dealing with the world, so the mastery of "good deportment" is not sufficient for the corporeal manifestation of the Unconditioned in the realm of the conditioned. The permeability of the form of the body demanded in the symbol of the Absolute is something else and means more than the physical form of behavior suited to a community or to a job.

What does this mean: the body which we are? It means the human being, the whole human being as a person as he not only experiences himself, but, as embodied, expresses himself. One cannot be aware of the body only at an objective distance as the body that one *has*, and of which one can be conscious as a thing, or use as an instrument to perform in the world. One can and should be inwardly aware of what one calls the body as the body that one *is*. This is the body as a *Gestalt*, graspable by the senses, in which I as a person am *there* in the world, am corporeally perceived by my fellow men, and myself perceive them.

Understood in this way, the body is the totality of the movements and attunements through which the human being feels, expresses, and presents himself as the person simultaneously conscious of himself, experiencing and acting in the world, who persists or passes away in space and time, and who actualizes or fails to actualize his true self.

Not only "inwardly," but also as embodied, visibly and concretely *there* as a person in the world, is one on the right path or not, equal to the situation or not, strong or weak, in equilibrium or off balance, open towards life or closed to it, in touch or with one's defenses up, in tune or out of phase, clear or dim, with or without "radiance," as a friend or an enemy – in short in harmony with one's true being or not! As embodied, one recognizes oneself as truly or inauthentically "there," whatever the current demands of the inner or outer situation are. One is truly there when one is embodied in such a way as to be open to one's essential being, i.e., to the way in which life may take form and manifest itself in our individuality here and now, at this very moment. One is inauthentically there to the extent that one, as embodied, here and now hinders the becoming and manifesting of one's essential Gestalt.

Once one has become conscious of the possibility and the task of transforming one's being-embodied in this way, a new life begins, for this task then accompanies all life-situations. The body which we are reflects in sayings and contradictions the heavenly and earthly origin of man. So there is a way of being embodied that with its warm and abundant aura and in the radiance of its essentially permeable form bears glorious testimony to the heavenly origin of man. And there is that other way of being there, conditioned by alternating cramped contraction and release, that reflects the egocentrically determined earthly origin of man. Only one who relates the law of this life to its heavenly origin will want to explain and excuse the interplay between egocentric rigidity and free-floating dissolution, not as the mere consequence of unfavorable circumstances, but will rather experience it as a co-responsible reaction to the determination promised and imposed by one's own nature.

Three Kinds of Body-Conscience

On the inner path, one can only make progress with the body if one is able to hear and follow the voice of the third kind of body-conscience. The first body-conscience is "self-preservation" and is concerned with health and efficiency of functioning in the world. The second body-conscience is oriented towards beauty, proportion, and the fulfilling of our Gestalt in every movement and activity in the world. However, the third body-conscience is the Great Permeability, the being transparent for our immanent transcendence. A human being can in this sense be in "Olympic" form, sound to the core, capable of almost superhuman feats, also beautiful in the strength of his body, and yet far removed from transparency; and one who is on the point of death can be in perfect bodily condition, open to the approaching other *life* that will transform him in death.

We can injure our transparency through something that harms neither our health nor our "figure," for example, by "a little too much" at a mealtime or by what above all hinders the progress of young people on the inner path, more than is usually thought – namely, self-satisfaction. This last takes away the radiance, i.e., the expression of an existence true to its essence; and therapists who encourage self-satisfaction in their patients as something quite natural that is proscribed only by outdated taboos, are totally ignorant of this radiance and the essential being that appears in it. It is questionable to what extent onanism is detrimental to health. That it goes against nature is beyond question. The feeling of guilt that accompanies it can, insofar as it has moral grounds, be overplayed – but not insofar as the voice of one's own essence speaks from it!

Transparency for transcendence as the meaning of practice seeks "the healing power of pure gesture," in which man is undistorted for Being in the personal expression of his fullness, righteousness and unity. But the man who is transparent in the right way mirrors, simply by his way of being there, the whole triunity of Being.

Work on the embodied transparency of human being presupposes knowledge of many things, both with respect to what hinders this transparency and to the possibility of transforming given hindrances into bodily permeability. Normal gymnastics has nothing to do with this. Physical exercises have long been oriented towards a notion of the "healthy body." In cases where gymnastics includes beauty and gracefulness, this still generally happens in a secular sense, although it may be a gateway to the awareness of initiatory possibilities.

In the human being who is almost exclusively oriented towards the world – towards his performance in and his impression on the world – there must first, above all, arise the sense for what it means to be open in body to the divine Being that resides in us – and not only in solemn gesture! – and to the bodily prerequisites for such openness.

The decisive prerequisite is the anchoring of the body in the true center. Connected with this are correct breath and correct tone.

The Relation of Man to Above and Below, to the World and to Himself

From the physical appearance of the human being, from out of the body which he "is," three things speak to us:

1. A certain relation to "the Above" and "the Below": man cannot fly, nor is he compelled to crawl. He is neither bird nor worm, but as human he carries himself upright, i.e. elevated towards heaven on the earth.
2. A certain connection with the world: man stands in a polar relationship to the world, in which he on the one hand maintains himself, and on the other is bound to the world in a bond of vital reciprocation.
3. A certain relation to himself: in whatever form he has become, he always stands in a definite relation to the life that in him presses towards manifestation, evolution and unification.

The essential being of man always presses towards a form in which it can manifest in the world. Where this is possible, man is in his center. Man's "being-in-his-center" is never anything only inner, but also has to do with man in his existence in the world, i.e., as embodied.

The Gestalt, i.e., the way a human being is there, is therefore "right" if in it he is transparent for his essential being and the Being present in his essence. This transparency is given and guaranteed only in a quite definite relation of man to above and below, to the world and to himself. However, man's being this way, conditioned by the current inner and outer circumstances, never completely corresponds to the inner image of the right relationship. Man is therefore always only on the way to the total Gestalt that has been entrusted to him and focused in the true center.

1. Whether man is in tune with respect to the relationship between heaven and earth is above all noticeable in his "comportment", i.e., in the way in which he embodies the verticality destined to him as man in contrast to the animals. Is this not a symbol of his heavenly origin? If he is "upright" in the right way, then in his behavior he connects heaven and earth. His connection to below does not jeopardize his being upright, and there is in his being upright no denial of his connection with the earth. He is rather in touch with a Below that, like the root structure of a tree, does not contradict upward movement but rather produces and ensures it. At the same time, his striving upwards does not have the character of a movement that pulls him away from the earth but rather of an upward movement that testifies to the life-giving power of roots. Man's "upright" appearance with respect to the relationship between heaven and earth expresses in an undistorted and harmonious way that he is simultaneously grounded in the earth and related to heaven, nourished and supported by the earth and attracted towards heaven, bound to the earth and yet striving upward towards heaven.

2. If the living Gestalt is in the proper relationship to the world, human beings, things and nature this means that man is both closed and open to the world, simultaneously clearly outlined against and yet in fluid contact with it, separated from the world and yet bound to it, reserved and at the same time open to the world. As a properly vital Gestalt, he both constantly inhales the world into himself and peacefully exhales himself into it.

3. If the living Gestalt displays the right relationship of man to himself, he then appears both controlled and relaxed, both in a self-maintaining form and also animated by a vital dynamism and in the right proportions of contraction and expansion.

Thus, the right Gestalt appears in the triad of posture, breath, and tone.

With respect to the three forms in which the right relationship to heaven and earth, to the world and to oneself appears, we can now see in what way and to what extent the human being who has not yet found or has again lost his center, is injuring the law inherent in his nature in a form appropriate to it. Every failure to respond to one's basic dictates manifests as a disturbance of the equilibrium between two poles, whether as a preponderance of heaven over earth or of earth over heaven, of the ego over the world or the world over the ego, of the form over the life immanent in it or of life over the form that serves its manifestation.

1. So we see people who wrong their natural relation to heaven and earth in that, in their standing, sitting, and walking, they either exaggerate it by straining upwards or else they sag downwards in such a way as to extinguish all sense of the dimension between above and below. In the latter case, instead of being supported by the earth in a vital way, they give the impression of lifeless inertia and depression. Being grounded in roots appears as burdensome heaviness, having a foundation as a sticking to the ground. Such people do not walk but drag themselves along; they do not stand but just manage to keep from collapsing.

If the upward tendency gains the upper hand, the person functions as if being constantly pulled upwards, in such a way as to deny all relation to the below. These people walk, stand, or sit with their bodies straining upwards. In walking, they never plant their feet on the ground but rather bounce, trip, and skip along. They deny their natural weight. They do not stand upright in a natural way, but with tensely raised shoulders are "distorted" upwards. Thus, their functioning is always cramped, inflated or "high-flown."

In both cases, the center that connects above with below, the right point of balance, is lost. If this can be found, then the forces that point towards heaven and affirm the earth are brought into the harmony of the whole. Whatever is on top is supported by what is below. Whatever is below has a natural tendency towards the above. The form grows from below to above as with the tree, and the top rests on a vertical stem that has broad and deep roots. Correct posture expresses man's affirmation of his wholeness, spanning heaven and earth. He does not cling to the earth but rather relys on it. He strives towards heaven, but does not forget his earth.

2. The lack of the right relation to the world shows in behavior in which the person either is not open to the world that approaches him and closes himself off from it or else appears totally subjected to it. In the first case the person does not function as a whole but is blocked off. He functions, not as a living contour, but hardened, numbed, and unanimated in his features. He is without contact like a lifeless figure. His reticence is not the expression of a natural, free distance but of a defensive contraction. He no longer functions as a Gestalt pulsing with vital breath but as an unanimated form that is completely contracted into itself. He does not flow in the living relation between I and Thou. He does not breathe in the vital rhythm of holding and letting go, of giving and retaining, of letting in and giving forth. He lacks the attitude that inclines and, at the same time, opens and connects itself to the world.

The opposite picture is one in which every kind of restraint is lacking. The gestures of such people manifest an unstable surrender to the world, in which they throw themselves into it with total abandon and thereby let it threaten to swallow them up. Nothing holds the Gestalt together. The strength to create distance or to withstand is lacking. The person dissolves into his surroundings, giving the impression of imminent disintegration. People of this sort move as if they had no bones in their bodies, as if nothing were holding them together. They are generally also tactless, lacking any sense of distance.

As in the previous case, the right center is lacking. They have no center of gravity to enable them either to stand independently or to connect with themselves or the world. Man's authentic relation to the world can be realized only in the creatively balanced tension between the poles. World and self must always be able to stand independently and yet be related and bound to one another.

They must also be able to separate, in order to be able to find themselves and unite again, in order to win themselves anew in this union. The right relationship, i.e., man's proper way of relating to the world, consists primarily in an attitude characterized by inclination, connectedness and openness, yet not by surrender. In his relation to the world man appears "in his center" if his constitution imperturbably allows the eternal in and out of the breath, in which he pours himself into the world without losing himself in it, remains in it without being swallowed up, can retire without cutting himself off from it, and can remain in himself without atrophying.

3. Man lacks the right relation to himself wherever there is an imbalance between the inner life and the form that has been attained, whether manifesting as an overwhelming outpouring of the inner life or as an over-atrophied or constraining form.

There are people whose appearance always gives the impression that their inner life is overflowing to the extent that it threatens to annihilate any kind of form.

Such people function totally on feeling, formlessly, without direction or order. Their movements are without proportion, unrhythmical, uncontrolled and uncoordinated.

In the opposite case, the generous flow of vital movement is lacking. Their gestures are stiff and inhibited, and when they are still, it is as if the Gestalt has collapsed into itself. One has no sense of the inner core that moves and animates the totality, holds it together organically and vitally radiates from it. The totality seems arbitrarily thrown together and seems as if it could at any moment suddenly explode or collapse.

In summary the inner life can be stronger than the shell containing it, or else the shell constrains the inner life. The "inner life" can mean two things: the natural energies of fundamental forces, or else life that instead of being lived has been pushed down into the unconscious – the shadow side. The shell then functions as an armor that stifles all life. In both cases the concentrating and unfolding center is lacking, in which the contradiction between the form that has been attained and the inner life is constantly resolved. If the center is there, the person's appearance becomes an undistorted expression of the inner life, and it functions as a harmonious dynamism. Form and life are no longer in opposition but work together. The form functions in a way neither affected nor sluggish, neither disintegrated nor rigid, but rather in such a way as to maintain and yet constantly form itself – simply living. From moment to moment the inner life fulfills itself in an appropriate form, and correspondingly the form renews itself in constant transformation from the life that bodies forth in it. At every moment the person's appearance is an expression and result of a creatively renewing and constantly resolving life. All the limbs seem to be harmoniously moved and animated from an indestructible center, charged with vital energy. The totality is relaxed form – formed relaxation.

Just as the lack of the proper center always means a disturbance of the vital totality, so the proper center means nothing other than a constitution in which the totality vitally maintains itself in the relational tension between the poles! Where the center is lacking, the person falls from one extreme into the other. One who is inflated sooner or later crumples, and one who has collapsed is periodically pulled back up to the other extreme. The person lacking a center alternates in his behavior towards the world between defensive distance and total abandonment, and one who is not in relation to himself oscillates between spasmodic contraction and disintegration.

The bodily Gestalt is the expression of the total human constitution. So too, the true center of gravity, whether or not one is in a position to localize it in a particular place in the body, is always a characteristic of the person's total constitution, which manifests in body *and* in soul. The true center of gravity that manifests in bodily as well as in psycho-spiritual behaviour is therefore an expression of a third thing. What is this third thing? Precisely the *total* human being, who as a "person in becoming" finds himself in a constitution true to his nature, aligned with the world, and also in never ending transformation.

If one talks of the total human being, this means something different from the ordinary point of view than from the initiated point of view.

The relation of man to above and below, to the world and to himself, manifests differently in the ordinary person whose fulfillment lies in proper existence and performance in the world, than in the initiated person, whose whole life is conditioned by the committed relation to immanent transcendence and who in the middle of his finite existence bears testimony to its infinite origin.

The relation to heaven and earth manifests in the upright posture given only to man. In this is symbolized the relationship of spirit and matter. But this signifies something different for the ordinary than for the initiated person. For the former, "the above," being directed and aimed upwards, means the predominance of the waking, rational, and value-oriented spirit over the "dark" realm of the impulses. For the initiated person, uprightness signifies the energy that spiritualizes the earth. This appears as a vibrating radiant light that permeates the body and attests to its transcendental nature and origin, as opposed to which, in the sphere of the ordinary person, the whole body never overcomes a certain heaviness, a denseness, and a definite lack of radiance, even when within his horizon he maintains himself "spiritually" and feels and fulfills himself happily. The initiated person, or more appropriately, the person, if and to what extent he is in the initiatory relationship, has a fluidity, an aura, and conveys the presence of a mysterious Third that is by no means given with the perfected personality in the worldly sense. On the other hand, no person, not even one well advanced on the initiatory path, is able to maintain himself in this presence continuously. When he lapses from it, he immediately loses the radiance peculiar to him which manifests the presence of the "higher," of heaven.

In the relation of man to the world, the right relation to other people and to the environment does not mean the same for the ordinary person as for the initiated. For the former, contact fulfills the prerequisites for a secure life, a meaningful existence, and a secure place in the community – and so corresponds to the three main desires of the ordinary ego. For the initiated person, contact means feeling at one with one's nature, which ultimately grants the experience of indestructible life, meaning, and safety independent of security, justness and community in the worldly sense.

Man's relation to himself, seen only in the light of the ordinary person, means the relation of the self-conscious, ego conscious of the world to the "personal unconscious", which is conditioned by the person's character and biography. For the initiated person on the other hand, the decisive theme is the relation of the conscious ego to the archetypal background that lies in the "collective unconscious" and between the ego conditioned by the world, the body that has developed under its destined conditions in the world, and the unconditioned essence that yet strives towards its form through all the conditions of the world.

Maturity and Immaturity in the Body

Wherever Being itself manifests in our existence, its triunity is manifested also. Even in its pragmatic aspect, the body mirrors this triunity: abundance as physical energy, law as more or less perfected "structure" in its symmetry and in its harmony, in rest as in motion, and unity in its openness for physical contact. Thus, all pragmatic education of the body stands under the manifestation of this triunity of Being. The initiated person, however, experiences in embodiment, as the medium of transcendence, the triunity of Being, as a mysterious abundance of "*Life*" numinously flowing through him and as a transcendental power even in the midst of physical weakness and outer emptiness. He experiences law, even in the midst of physical illness, as a bright well-being and as a strangely harmonious situation in the midst of worldly discord; and the unity of Being is experienced in a numinous feeling of bodily belonging to a cosmic body that is in and around us, in which indeed we are and breathe beyond ourselves like waves in the ocean. To the extent that we become transparent, we experience ourselves as the body which we are, in its physical participation in a totality that animates and transcends us: that is our human destiny, to manifest each in our individual way!

In order to attain permeability of the body which we are, a long period of maturation is necessary. "Bodily maturity" in the initiatory sense is different from biological maturity. The potential fruit of this latter maturity is the child. The fruit of maturity in the initiatory sense is rebirth from out of the essence presupposed by the Great Permeability.

The mature person is "relaxed in form," for he has released his ego and is centered in his essence. In his whole bearing he is not dependent on support from the world or on recognition by others. He is calm in himself; his being-embodied, his way of being *there*, is an expression of his inner freedom which is independent of the world. The mature person's self-consciousness comes not from a secure position but from his being rooted in something beyond the world. Lack of maturity in the body appears most clearly as tenseness alternating with looseness, depending on the circumstances. The mature person is neither tense nor loose, but in his soul as in his body, he is both supple and in form. He is in form and does not fall out of form. But this form, however compact, is not closed off; however open, is not abandoned. If a person is truly on the path, he is immediately conscious of every loosening and every tension, not only because it causes pain or injures his physical condition – also not only because it prevents his functioning properly – but because he automatically becomes aware of it as the sign of a distortion of what he authentically is and will be. He feels himself blocked from contact with his essence. And he will experience every looseness just as much as every tension, hardening, and atrophying, as being wrong – not only because he does not feel well in it and no proper attitude to world and work is possible, but because it denies him the form appropriate to his essence. The sign of the success of spiritual practice is that one feels oneself more in one's body, i.e., with more energy, in better form and contact, and all this quite independently of all current circumstances in the world. A spiritual practice that does not give that would have no power to transform man.

Hara

The body as the medium of expression of the person speaks to us in *posture* (which is determined by the centre of gravity), in *breath*, and in the relationship of *tension* and *relaxation*. All three concepts do not, personally understood, mean anything corporeal, but are rather media for the expression of the personal possibilities of proper (that means appropriate to one's essence) existence and becoming – or the prevention of this.

When the body is understood as the unity of the attitudes in which the person is there in the world and as the medium of personal self-realization, which is in fact only possible from a transcendental root, disturbances of the body are never merely physical disruptions but reflect a disturbance of the essence and the orientation of the whole human being. Work on the body, which is as much a part of the initiatory path as it is of personal therapy, is something other than medical treatment.

Disturbances of the body, looseness and tension in particular, are manifestations of inappropriate attitudes of the person. So, for example, tension signifies inflated ambition and vanity or else a self-abasing attitude of anxiety or lack of confidence; sudden loosening means not only physical exhaustion, but also, for example, discouragement and disappearing self-confidence.

Let us take as an example a tensing of the shoulder musculature. This can never be properly understood if one sees in it only physical tension, which one could deal with by means of massage, relaxation exercises, or even an injection if necessary, since it is always co-conditioned, if not wholly caused, by an inner maladjustment. From the personal point of view, the same phenomenon means something else. In the hunched up shoulders there appears the predominance of the little ego that needs security and has a lack of trust of the world and of life that comes from a lack of self-consciousness.

It becomes clear that all maladjustments and the resulting physical disturbances are basically signs of an ego that pressures man out of the fullness of life and causes him to loose his essential roots.

The person enclosed in his ego has an inborn distrust of the next moment. He is always beset by some kind of worry or crisis. He can never let anything just come to him and always unconsciously thinks that at the time of an examination, for example, he must once again "do" what he basically already can do, something that is even easily at his disposal, if he could only let it come out at the appropriate time. Since, owing to a lack of self-confidence, he is unable to do this, when it comes down to it – he fails, he "does it again."

The personal handling of such a maladjustment goes beyond the seeing and experiencing of the attitude that expresses and inculcates security and trust. Instead of upwards tension, one needs anchoring to below, getting down to the pelvic region, where this is not seen from without as a part of the body. It must rather be understood as the decisive medium for actualizing the way in which one is *there* in the world as a whole human being, right or wrong, open or closed off. Understood in this way, it is a center, whose proper development can mean an eventual relaxed security owing to an experiential connection to a more embracing power. It thereby fulfills, beyond its pragmatic usefulness, its initiatory meaning.

Just as the human being cannot be understood as a person, unless with respect to his transcendental determination, in the same way the *personally* correct way to see and to exercise the body which one is, is to let it develop, with respect to its significance as a medium of the maturation of the total human being, into transparency for transcendence. Man is then only properly there when he is there as a body in relation to his essential being, and therefore open for the corporeal manifestation of his essence.

Exercise of the body towards transparency means the dismantling of everything that stands in the way, and the furthering of everything that makes it possible. Hindrances to the manifestation of one's essence consist in any aspects of the ego in its attempts to maintain itself. Signs of this are tension and its opposite, release. Both are equally far removed from the correct way of being embodied. Every posture of the persona, every facade that hides one's true being, every false tone in the voice, every uncertainty in the eye, every artificiality or carelessness in the posture can and must be taken as symptoms of an insufficient anchoring in one's essence, and made conscious as a personal illness to be put aside in the *exercitium ad integrum*.

Man's correct posture is always determined by the correct "center of gravity." The bad posture of so many people consists in the displacement of the center of gravity to a point too high, accompanied by the attitude of "Chest out – stomach in." Such distortions of posture are the expression of a person who is completely identified with his small ego and therefore wants above all to ensure its position. Such posture blocks the loosening, renewing and sustaining power that comes from the depths. The opposite of this posture, often to be seen alternating with it, is the collapsing or crumpling together of the person. Here, the image of the upright man is distorted. Such flabbiness, where it is not simply a matter of physical exhaustion, betrays a lack of feeling and responsibility for the proper form, without which one's essential being cannot appear. A person can make progress towards the correct form only when he learns to be aware of the middle of his body, his belly, in the right way. It is admittedly at first somewhat surprising and puzzling for Western man to realize that the center of the body that is oriented towards transcendence; a center to be actualized and maintained, is the belly, more exactly the diaphragm and the pelvic cavity.

The significance of the belly, as we encounter it again and again in Romance and early Gothic representations of man, but also in portrayals of Christ as savior of the world, has long been recognized in the Orient, especially in Japan, where it plays an important role in the practice of maturity, i.e. integration with transcendence. In the sphere of Japanese culture we find it in the doctrine and practice of "*Hara.*"

Hara literally means "belly" and by extension that whole constitution of man in which he becomes more and more free from the spell of the small ego and is able in a relaxed way to anchor himself in a reality that enables him to feel life from elsewhere, to master the world and to serve indefatigably his task in the world. He can then fight, die, form, and love without anxiety.

Where the person is able to lower and anchor himself in the "Hara," he experiences it as a place of life-energy that is bound to him, through which he is able to see through the hardened ego forms, to take them up and to forge and transform them into new forms. Through this capability of transformation and renewal, he is able to take the world differently. Nothing upsets him, nothing can push him out of his vibrating equilibrium. His head remains cool, the whole body is relaxed yet toned, and the person breathes the breath of the center in the rhythm of opening and closing himself, giving and finding himself. He is able to remain calm amidst the "storm of the world." In the Hara, man rests in the source of never-ending transformation and thereby in the foundations of his own personal being and becoming. The Hara-no-hito, the person with a belly, means the mature person, who has attained the pre-requisite for the integration of the ego and the essence. Only the person who is able to descend from the sphere of the ego into the space of the Hara and anchor himself there, is ultimately able to reach his personal center.

The seeking and practicing of Hara, that fundamental center that simultaneously relaxes, supports, and makes us upright, is the basic exercise for all proper (i.e., adequate to our essence) "existence in the world." It is the practice in which the totality of belly, pelvic region and sacrum become the dependable foundation of correct posture. The practice of the relaxed and at the same time firm center makes all walking, standing, and sitting a sign of an existence true to its essence. The field for this practice is, in fact, the whole everyday world, for if in walking, standing, or sitting we forget Hara, our personal presence suffers. Whoever armors himself up in the realm of the ego remains closed off from his essence; whoever dissolves himself downwards is deprived, even where it touches him, of the form that would take him up.

There is no activity that demands our focused attention and concentrated will that does not jeopardize our holding the center, our existing in Hara. Wherever we exert ourselves in a goal-oriented way, fix on something from the point of view of the ego, we can easily lose our center. Every kind of work and goal-directed activity misleads us, if we are not practiced in Hara, into transposing our center of gravity too high, i.e., into doing everything with our ego. Precisely for that reason, *every* activity is an opportunity to practice correct posture. Every moment gives us occasion to maintain and strengthen that constitution which frees us from the domination of the ego, which is afraid of pain and needs security and affirmation, and lets us be from our essence. To the extent that we succeed in this, all our tasks will flow more easily. What we are able to do stands at our disposal, and in our commerce with other people we are relaxed, calm and free.

The shortest definition of Hara is as follows: Hara is the total constitution of man as body, which eliminates whatever stands in his way! This applies both to the person who lives as a personality in the world, and to the person on the path of initiation; for in both cases it is the little ego that stands in the way. Hara eliminates the embodied dominance of the little ego! Then, at the decisive moment, whatever one has, can do, and knows in the world is at one's disposal. In the case of illness, for example, the healing forces of nature are not distorted by the ego's anxiety, and whoever is able to dissolve the embodied tendencies of the ego in the Hara is underway on the inner path and free for the manifestation of Being in the body.

If we talk of the Hara as the right center, we thereby mean only the earth-center. Man's center is and remains the "Heart." There man finds himself, given that he has been able to free himself in the Hara from his centeredness in the ego. He finds himself then, as the child of heaven and earth, i.e., as the fruit of a maturation that fulfills itself in the union of earth (*Eros-Kosmos*) and heaven (*Logos*).

Just as centeredness in the ego confines man to the realm of the conditioned, and only liberation from the domination of the ego opens the gate to man's essential being, i.e., to the unconditioned, so also composure in the Hara opens the gate to the influx of a universal energy, in which man by his nature participates, but from which he is as a rule cut off. The Japanese call this energy "Chi," the universal energy in which we participate and which we must learn to cultivate in contrast to will-power. Where we are able to cultivate chi-energy, we are capable of untiring and varied performance, of which we would not be capable without chi.

---

[1]German has the advantage of two words for "body": "*Leib*" which means primarily a living, organic (usually human) body; and "*Körper*" which is used more for inert physical bodies, e.g., "the heavenly bodies." This distinction is difficult to carry over into English, but I shall sometimes use "embodiment" to suggest "*Leib*" as opposed to "*Körper*." – The Translator

HERBERT V. GUENTHER

Towards Spiritual Order

ALL around us and even within ourselves, we observe two powerful tendencies. The one is in the direction of order, though not in the sense of a static end-state but in that of an ongoing ordering process; the other is in the direction of disorder, into a state – and here the concept of "state" is appropriate – of randomness, of death. These two tendencies even seem to be of unequal strength, the tendency towards dissolution being the stronger one. After all, no one has escaped nor is anyone likely to escape this ultimate equilibrium state of maximum molecular disorder and uniformity, or maximum entropy, as one says in physics. This undeniable tendency, however, is valid only in the case of "closed" systems. But there is growing evidence that there are no closed systems, in the strict sense of the word, anywhere in the universe. Hence, it is nothing more than an assumption that this tendency is the only one operating in the universe. Yet this assumption, although it has become deeply ingrained in our thinking, because it applied to a class of processes that had been arbitrarily selected and systematically studied, is an expression of "ignorance", a limited view that we take as the only and ultimate one. However, if we turn away from the "studied ignorance" of theories that try to explain the phenomenon of life rather than to observe and to understand it, deep down within ourselves, we feel that this tendency is not the only one, that it is a special instance in the sense that it may be a powerful stimulus in the service of an overall development towards higher orders which are characterized by "knowledge." Of course, terms like "ignorance" and "knowledge" are "loaded" concepts; yet it is "knowledge,"

taken in the sense of the fact of human intelligence, which is operative at all levels, and there is no evidence that knowledge ever developed out of chaos by way of random fluctuations or by the agency of an extramundane power. Such an assumption, despite the fact that it is widely held, is as insipid as the claim, which is not made but should have been made on the basis of this kind of reasoning, that health is an outcome of disease. Actually, it is the other way round: disease is a loss of health, and chaos is an indication that something has gone wrong. Therefore, when we find ourselves in a chaotic situation in which we have lost our bearings and which is so aptly called Samsāra – running around in circles – this state, far from being an end-state, is more like a danger signal drawing our attention to the fact that something has to be done about it. Paradoxically, Samsāra is on the whole favorable to – let us say, spiritual – growth and development. But how can this be? Samsāra is said to be frustration and suffering, generating further frustration and added suffering. The answer to this question is, first of all, not to allow ourselves to be hypnotized into this apparent aspect as the only one possible but to look at the immediate facts with eyes that can "see" instead of merely registering. To see is impossible without, and even presupposes, "intelligence" operating within life.

Once it is recognized that Samsāra, in which we seem to have been caught unawares through "ignorance," is more like a danger signal and not an inevitable situation or condition of human life, the question of how something has gone wrong naturally arises. This very question already contains the answer that there was no necessity for such a happening and that, apart from this occurrence, something can be done about it. It is like a case of catching a cold: there is no necessity to do so, but once it has happened that I have caught a cold, I can do something about it and be restored to health. Similarly, something can be done about "ignorance," which is more like a disease, a local irregularity in a larger field.[1]

The restoration of ourselves to health, the progression from "ignorance" to "knowledge," is a delicate procedure that cannot be rushed without grave dangers, and it is for this reason that a preparatory phase is emphasized, which often has involved the misunderstanding of this phase as an end in itself. It must be understood that the preparatory phase is not an isolated event but a complex situation in which it dawns upon a person that something must be done and that, at the same time, assistance is needed. This complex situation is aptly summarized by Klong-chen rab-'byams-pa:[2]

> Just as a patient is in need of a physician,
> People of a ruler, a lonely traveller of an escort,
> A merchant of a guild-master, a boatsman of a boat,
> So in order to calm the emotions, to make evil harmless,
> To overcome birth and death, to have the bitendential values of Being spontaneously present, and
> To cross the ocean of fictitious being, you must rely on a teacher.
> Do so with four positive ideas in mind,
> Since in so doing all other methods are outweighed.
> The teacher is the physician, his instruction the medicine,
> You yourself the patient,
> Your effort the application of the medicine,
> And peace and happiness, the result of having got rid of the illness.

There is a deeper message in this statement. Apart from restating the indubitable fact that health is primary and illness a deviation from this state, it focuses attention on the teacher who, like a physician in the best sense, can only act as a catalyst to our individual effort. Without this effort, nothing whatsoever will be achieved. This is to say that it is in us to grow healthy again. In this way, the preliminary phase in which we become aware of being ill links up with the "actual procedure" of restoring ourselves to health. The "preliminary" phase may look and even feel unpleasant and dangerous: after all, "growth" is like a journey that has many vicissitudes. It is a move into an as yet unknown territory, and it is the "before" (the preliminary) that may frighten us, while the "actual" journey of exploration may be pure joy. On the other hand, the preliminary phase may as well be a protective measure. This ambivalence between danger and precaution is admirably brought out in the following passage:[3]

> "While before one sets out on a dangerous mountain path, the area may seem to be infested with bandits and robbers, the actual going may be without anxiety and fear. Or, the preliminary phase may be like the fortification by moats and so on of a border town so that an enemy has no chance to intrude. So also in this case here, by having made a preliminary, the hordes of Samsāra are repelled."

There is, of course, an intimate relationship between the preliminary and preparatory phase and the actual procedure. Not only is the one meaningless without the other, but to ignore this relationship may well lead to disaster:

> "The preliminary is like an efficient escort, the actual procedure is like a wealthy man who has been freed from his fears. However, if there is no escort, even if there be a special procedure, one had better not set out on a dangerous journey without an escort; because if one were to do so, one might be overpowered by enemies. On the other hand, even if there is an escort, but no travellers, there is no point for the escort to set out on a journey.

Similarly, if there is no content (meaning) in the actual procedure, whatever preparations are made, they will bear no fruit. Thus the preliminary and preparatory phase and the actual procedure must go together, since thereby the aspirant will realize his goal."[4]

The preliminary is in the service of regaining one's health, which is not merely physical but much more spiritual. Therefore, in order to regain this state "beyond frustration and suffering," we have to become aware of and deeply feel the unsatisfactory situation of Saṃsāra in which we are ordinarily involved and which we perpetuate by our, mostly inconsiderate, activities, be they of the bodily, verbal, or mental variety. It is these that have to be scrutinized and to be transmuted from mere impulsiveness and compulsiveness into the meaningfulness of existence, into communication which conveys its message without argument or ideal proliferation of words, and into the clarity of pristine cognitiveness which is appreciative rather than a restless drive for novelties. In order to be able to do so, one must become a "vessel," as the Buddhist texts assert. The symbolism is clear: before we can grow, we must have become receptive of the forces that aid growth. Not only that, the "vessel" must be clean, and hence the cleansing of the vessel is a preparatory act which involves the dismissal of all ego-centered concerns, which on the overt level are the obsession with ritual and on the inner level the imaginative flight into beliefs about oneself which will not withstand a critical assessment and which ultimately merely reinforce our dividedness against ourselves and are unable to heal the split which is the root of our suffering.

If the preliminary phase is properly lived through and not merely dispassionately contemplated, it fuses with the actual procedure or growth; even before this fusion as a many-faceted process, it climaxes in a phase that is marked by our being no longer divided against ourselves. There are seven facets involved, each leading to a higher-order awareness. They are summed up in the ostensibly simple statement:

"The exercise of transitoriness, compassion, and ethical awareness."[5]

But the key-terms "exercise" and "ethical awareness" are so rich in connotation that a satisfactory translation is almost impossible. "Exercise" is not only the employment of a faculty, it is much more a process of refinement, of harmonizing feeling and thinking. "Ethical awareness" is the positive purpose towards which man can drive forward, inasmuch as it is structured in terms of value and meanings, and therefore it prevents man from degenerating into a thoughtless robot. It is more than an "enlightened attitude," which is a relatively correct translation of the Indian term *bodhicitta*. In its Tibetan rendering *byang-(chub-kyi) sems*, it has been understood by the Tibetans as a concern with limpid clearness (*byang*) and consummate perspicacity (*chub*), which underlies all man's striving towards life's meaning and is never a euphoric state of oblivion but is an active process "made explicit through ethical actions reinforced by ethical judgments."[6]

It is significant that from among the seven facets of the preliminary phase, transitoriness is mentioned first as indispensible for every subsequent step. Transitoriness goes counter to our ingrained habits of thinking that at least some part of ourselves will outlast everything else. We may agree to the observable fact that everything is impermanent, but as a rule this agreement, if some feeling should be involved, is little more than cheap sentimentality. The reason why we instinctively refuse to apply impermanence to ourselves is that, from earliest childhood onwards, we have learned to detect (if not construe) certain invariant relationships between what we see and what we hear, between cause and effect, and many other operations and movements which all become "mapped" and which set up the "habitual standpoint," in which one more or less confuses the general structural features of our mental "maps" with features of the world.[7] "The map begins to interpret what is perceived in such a way that it seems to be an inevitable and necessary feature of the whole experience, so obvious that it is very difficult to question its basic features."[8] This invariance (permanence) is particularly strong with our cherished "ego," and since we have learned to "undo things," we are lulled into the belief that "undoing" cannot happen to us. To the extent that this facet of transitoriness is brought home to us, it serves as a powerful stimulus to look for new relationships which will generate the growth of a fresh understanding. In a certain sense, it becomes a search for invariance in the other direction or, as the texts state, to turn one's mind away from Saṃsāra.[9]

Klong-chen rab-'byams-pa, who is unique in the long history of Tibetan Buddhism because of his comprehensive view of the problems involved in man's spiritual growth, orders impermanence in three "layers" which as "external", "outward" or "public" relate to time; as "internal", "inward" or "private" relate to "space", not so much as occupied by something, but as something displaying its space, the live organism built up by the elemental forces that have shaped the individual as well as his environment; and as "secret", "hidden", not so obvious as the external or internal, relate to the intangible world of felt relationships exemplified by our parents and friends. Most important, impermanence must be realized as pertaining to ourselves, before we think of the rest of the universe in terms of impermanence. From a practical point of view, this procedure is like shock-therapy, jolting us out of our complacency. Klong-chen rab-'byams-pa's words may be quoted in full:[10]

"Externally, there is the change of the four seasons, revealing their impermanence day and night, from moment to moment; internally, there is the change occurring in our physiological make-up constituted by the four elemental forces and quickly disintegrating and having no solid core, like a cluster of bubbles; and "secretly," there is the death of our parents and relatives. This situation applies to us as well. There is no guarantee that we may not die this moment; every moment we should firmly impress on our mind the possibility that we may die tonight or tomorrow. Looking at other living beings, we note that none of them escapes the above conditions. (The next step) is to have the uncertainty of death present in our thinking. Thereby, the impermanence of all that has been constructed is realized and, once we start directing our mind to the immediate task of growing up spiritually, this constitutes the degree of refinement we have achieved through the practice of this first phase."

Anyhow, awareness of impermanence is made even more poignant when we turn to the world of feelings which in a sense constitutes our links with others. Feelings of happiness, however fleeting they may be, are infectious. They radiate into the environment which for us as living beings is not primarily made up of things, but of meanings. Each peron's world represents that person's horizon of meaning which he or she then concretizes into "things" and "places" which yet retain something of their original meaning, as when this concretized world is still termed "heaven" or "hell." The happiness we see in the eyes of a beloved person is as much the happiness we feel in ourselves. But we also note how quickly happiness passes and gives way to sorrow, which deeply distresses us. In the same way as illness is a loss of health and forces us to try everything possible to restore our health, so also sorrow is a loss of happiness and can be seen as a stimulus to do something about this situation and to banish the disturbing element from our being. One way of doing so is to realize the futility that attaches to "worldly concerns" which for most people is what traditional religions have called a "life in heaven."

Klong-chen rab-'byams-pa sees "heaven" and "hell" as alternating phases, temporary surface phenomena that lose their attraction and compelling power by a look behind the scenes. Or, even at the danger of being misunderstood by having to use anthropomorphic images, we can rid ourselves of these temporary scenes in our life by becoming the stage-director instead of being satisfied with merely being the puppets in the show:

". . . the heights and depths of Samsāra are like the buckets in a water-mill, in constant rotation. Apart from enlightenment which is release and the reliable means not to become involved in Samsāra, everything else does not allow the mind to become stabilized and merely confuses it. If one sets out on the road to freedom, one finds temporary happiness, and a life in heaven and positive qualities are planted in one's life-process as illustrated by the Bodhisattvas, the Buddha's spiritual sons; and ultimately lasting happiness and unsurpassed enlightenment are realized, as is illustrated by the Buddhas."[11]

The cold rationality of the "knowledge" of the world and the order of things in their impermanence is softened by the sensibility in feelings that remain inaccessible to the intellect and yet widen a person's horizon of this world, while simultaneously and subtly determining the manner and quality – the inseparable companion of meaning – of man's actions. This new dimension is not additive, despite the fact that a "multitude of conditions" is recognized. These conditions are rather an incentive to allow man's truly spiritual property, "compassion," to shine forth. Compassion nestles in the heart of each of us, although only too often it is not allowed to take the lead in human affairs and therefore is turned into its travesty, for the effect of uninformed sentimentality – one even has the lurking suspicion that it is its purpose – is to keep the object in its weak and inferior state. True compassion is rooted in the awareness that there are few circumstances which assist man in finding what he wants – happiness, pleasures, health and wealth – while there are many that militate against man's being successful in this pursuit and have him only more deeply immersed in frustration. Klong-chen rab-'byams-pa lists as instances of such frustration the following:[12]

"Even if one has helped another person, instead of being helped in return, one is harmed. Food and drink turn into causes of illness and death. The wealth one has accumulated rouses the concupiscence of enemies and thieves. When one is in need, the person whom one has thought to be one's friend, turns into an implacable enemy. Even if one has done no harm, one is slandered and vilified baselessly. Whatever one may do, one will not please the other."

And so compassion is roused by the distress that is felt when one sees oneself and others ever and again slip into what leads us away from ourselves.

Although compassion makes us aware of the ties that connect us with the rest of the living universe, it does not tell us how we have to respond to the challenge it presents to us. It is true, somehow we have an inkling that friendliness makes for better relationships than hostility, but there is always the preoccupation with the devious demands by the ego, which acts more as a barrier towards understanding than as an aid for assessing the prevailing situation. Because of this conflict within ourselves, the importance of a teacher is impressed upon us. In this context, a teacher is not so much a person who imparts cumulative knowledge but one who guides us to ourselves and awakens us to an awareness or knowledge that is existential. Existential awareness is not a mood (and hence it has little to do with the pseudo-philosophy of existentialism). It is grounded in the very nature of Being, irreducible to the categories of rational (and not-so-rational) thought, though making them possible. In the last analysis it is this existential awareness that speaks to us from within ourselves through the "teacher." Here it is necessary to sound a warning. The little word "within" is treacherous in that it can lull us into the belief that since the "ego" is within and the rest of the universe "without," all that is necessary is to listen to and to follow the idiosyncrasies of the ego. Moreover, it is alleged that listening to someone else also involves a dependent relationship which "makes me weak." Such is the perversity of ego-centric thinking, that it will reject a "teacher" but accept a "guru." Literally this Sanskrit word means "heavy," "weighty," literally as well as figuratively. In addition, it also has the connotation of "arduous," "difficult to bear," "venerable" and "respectable." It is perhaps this latter connotation that has given rise to the spread of the "cult" of the guru which, on closer inspection, reconfirms an escapist attitude. It is enough to sit at the feet of the "master" with a little imitation thrown in for good measure. The other connotations of difficulty, weightiness and demandingness are conveniently overlooked. Yet it is patent that if no demands are made which are aimed at us to rouse us from our lethargy, nothing will be done. It is only natural that, as a rule, we feel uncomfortable if demands are made on us. On the one hand, they disturb the placidity and the routine we have adopted in going about our daily life, and on the other hand, they show us or, to put it more strongly, confront us with an aspect of ourselves which for the most part we do not like to see, simply because we would have to do something about it. In this sense, the guru is a mirror which is not so much a mere mechanical reflector but a powerful revealer of our nature or our being to ourselves. This "inner" nature that is now revealed on the "outside" has been lying dormant; it has been neglected and its neglect has had us starved in the barrenness of our own fictions about ourselves and about the environment of which each of us is a constitutive part. The demands which the guru as a mirror of ourselves makes on us are a "heavy" burden. But once we realize that we ourselves are this "burden," its heaviness gives way to "lightness" because there is nothing to restrict the openness of Being or even to weigh it, because it is not a thing relative to other things and because only mutual relativity can serve as a means of measurement.

The demands which the "teacher," be he a teacher, a friend, or a "guru," makes on us are not such that they cannot be executed. On the contrary, they make us turn to ourselves so as to develop, bring to light, let be the capabilities, qualities, capacities that are within us, not as narrowly defined and circumscribed "essences" but as properties and dynamic vectors of what is termed Buddhahood. This is not a static end-state, as such it would be only another form of stagnation. The term "Buddhahood" must be understood as a feeble attempt to describe, not to define rigidly and reductively, an experience that, from any ordinary point of view (which is riveted somewhere) is paradoxical – everything has gone (*sangs*) and yet everything has expanded (*rgyas*).[13] But where else can this experience be had, if not in and by the experiencer who is none else but the concrete human person? Naturally, this experience does not come easily; it needs tender care (bestowed on its development by the guru) and continuous effort (by the person who under the guidance of the guru exerts himself to let grow what is his very Being). As Klong-chen rab-'byams-pa puts it:[14]

"If one does not realize Buddhahood, there is no 'profit,' and if one does not pursue actively a path to realize Buddhahood, it will not be realized. Therefore, one has to pursue it by all means. One has to concentrate fully on the realization as was done by the marvelous *grub-thob*[15] of yore. They underwent many hardships. Just as they became free (from the conflict of Saṃsāra) by pursuing spiritual growth alone and in solitude, so also I shall dismiss from my mind the preoccupation with this life and realize life's meaning in solitude."

The emphasis on solitude implies no escape from the world, rather it suggests that we have first to "get ourselves into shape" so as to become more capable of dealing with the world which, as we have seen, is not a mere container, but is ourselves reflecting at every stage our "inner" state of order or disorder. Therefore, unless we "order" ourselves we will not find order anywhere else. The modern slogan of "law and order" is the height of absurdity – order can never be legislated; it can grow, just as a flower grows from its seed or a crystal from its nucleus.

The combination of effort on the part of the aspirant and of the message by the guru or teacher subtly brings about a change of attitude: because of the double role of the guru, being a person in the external world but also, figuratively speaking, being an inner prompting, the attitude turns from its concern with ephemeral things to something more abiding and to something that sustains life by endowing it with values. These values, the Buddha capabilities, are existential values intrinsic to Being, and not assigned values for an object that captivates the passing whim of the ego. Inasmuch as the awareness of values sees them as pertaining to the whole of the person striving for them, there occurs the first glimpse of a state in which no disorder, no dividedness against oneself, no playing one aspect of one's being against another (as is evident, to give only one example, in the contrast and conflict between the transcendental ego and the empirical ego) is possible. At the same time there is the awareness that the disregard of these values leads to illness. In the light of the importance of the guru who in his inner-outer role can even be understood as the self-regulatory principle of the system "human being," attention to it-him by tuning-in to the message sent out by him-it, becomes the very healing process we have been waiting for. In the words of Klong-chen rab-'byams-pa:[1]

"The captain who ferries us safely over the abysmal depth of the ocean of Saṃsāra is the guru, and the boat that is instrumental for doing so is the guru's instruction. Therefore, we have to take to heart what he says. Since and when we become afflicted with the disease of suffering by not heeding his advice, the guru as the king of physicians shows us his great kindness. Day and night we have patiently to take his medicine, that is, his instruction."

Such an awareness, once it becomes firmly rooted, serves as a solid armor against the fragmenting tendencies and the random state that characterize the world of the ego.[17]

This effort to preserve a non-divided state, which is made possible by the recognition of what dividedness means and does, is the last step in the preliminary and preparatory phase. Only from this safe ground is the actual process of spiritual growth possible. Because of its holistic character, it goes beyond and yet conquers what on the ordinary level is sharply contrasted as subject against object, self against other. In particular, this state is characterized as "pure pleasure" in which all judgments about its nature have been suspended. It is also felt as "radiating", both by ourselves and by others. We, too, express these moments of happiness, health and wholeness in terms of light – "glowing with happiness," "sparkling with joy," "radiating peace and calm." In these moments, we *are* the very meaning of life, because we are no longer barred from access to it. We have stepped over the wall we had erected out of fear. What has been achieved is the preservation of a flow-process which will go on towards ever higher levels which are the greater depth of our being, if left undisturbed.

The immediate effect of the practice of these preliminary exercises is that the conviction grows that one can do something about the situation in which we find ourselves. Since a situation implies that none of us is alone, this conviction also opens our eyes to the fact that there are others in the same plight as we ourselves, and this awareness evokes and takes on the character of compassion, of feeling with and for others. With the conviction that something can be done and with compassion for others present, the seed has been planted for becoming man – a person who is sure of the structure of his world, which he knows to extend into broader horizons and which he does not confuse with the island represented by his ego.

To effect this transition from being but another object or entity in a world made up of entities to being alive and open to meaning, it is necessary to change over from the ordinary way of thinking, which is representational and merely picks out these features of our experience of the world which are objectifiable and hence can be quantified and "measured" (numerically and quantitatively), to non-objectifying thinking in which (since an object has only meaning in relationship to a subject and where there is no object there also cannot be a subject in any meaningful sense) the subject–object structure is suspended. Non-objectifying, hermeneutical thinking releases thought from the compulsion to interfere and lets meanings present themselves in what appears before it. Such thinking retains vividness and pristineness and has to do with understanding. Such thinking is "a *path* or a *way* to an understanding of the world as a region of involvement. It uncovers not denotable object, although assuredly such denotations may accompany it, but rather the historical self-understanding of the experiencer as he is lodged in the world, advancing his projects amidst a welter of existential possibilities. Whereas representational thinking disengages itself from the experiencer and prescinds from his existentiality, bracketing him as a mere subject-pole so as to attend discriminately to the objective state of affairs, hermeneutical thinking attends to the existentiality of the experiencer and the historicality of the lifeworld."[18] Such hermeneutical thinking is termed *ye-shes* in Buddhist texts, and contrasted with *sems*, which in turn corresponds to our "mind" as a noetic-noematic complex operating in the subject–object framework. Its entitative status as such is questionable, because it is an emergent and not an absolute prius. Anything based on it, that is, to attend to its operation exclusively and to conduct one's life on its assumptions and constructs in the interest of measurement and control, leads to further confusion about what life means for a person who cannot be reduced to a lifeless abstraction. Whether we emphasize *ye-shes* or *sems*, the situationality of the experiencer is not abolished. In the former case, the situationality is the "Buddha-realms" (*zhing-khams*), each of them revealing distinct affinities with Being experienced as "existentiality" (*sku*) which, in phenomenological terms, is a "founding stratum" for the "pristine cognitions" (*ye-shes*) operating on it and ranging over the various "realms."[19] In the latter, it is our world of frustration, Saṃsāra. The complexity of situationality is, following the Buddhist analysis, made up of the "vision" of the experiencer, of his attending to this "vision," of his enacting this vision, and of the resultant from the above three modes. The situationality of random behavior by the experiencer who is engaged in ego-centered representational thinking is in marked contrast to the situationality of orderliness as is evident from experience, as expressed by dGa'-rab rdo-rje in the following words:[20]

> How emotionally tainted is the vision of one engaged in representational thinking;
> How deeply does his attention to this vision yield to despair;
> How toilworn becomes his life conducted in the mood of despair,
> How far astray does such a person go by expecting something to come out of it!

NOTES

[1] "Ignorance" is the lexical translation of *ma-rig-pa* in Tibetan and *avidyā* in Sanskrit and as such makes little sense, even if it is believed that such "translation" conveys meaning. We usually contrast "ignorance" with "knowledge" as irreconcilable states and separate entities. However, *ma-rig-pa* is not so much the opposite or contrary to *rig-pa* (an active process of bestowing meaning rather than of being merely receptive) but the stepped-down condition of the latter. It is a "loss" or reduction in the optimum level of performance. In Buddhist thought "knowledge," in the sense of a meaning-bestowing process, is basic to life, not an after-thought.

[2] *Kindly Bent to Ease Us*, Part One of the Trilogy of Finding Comfort and Ease (*ngal-gso skor-gsum*), translated and annotated by Herbert V. Guenther. (Emeryville, California: Dharma Publishing, 1975), p. 78.

[3] *Theg-pa'i mchog rin-po-che'i mdzod*, vol. II, p. 157.

[4] *Bla-ma dgongs-'dus*, vol. 9, p. 841 (= Ngagyur Nyingmay Sungrab, vol. 52).

[5] This concise statement which admirably sums up the Buddhist idea of growth is found in the *Sangs-rgyas-kyi 'das-rjes gsum*, a work included in the *Bi-ma snying-thig* (= *sNying-thig ya-bzhi*, vol. 7, p. 288) and repeatedly quoted in rNying-ma works. See, for instance, *mKha'-'gro snying-thig*, vol. 1, pp. 74 ff; *Bla-ma dgongs-'dus*, vol. 9, p. 519.

[6] *Kindly Bent to Ease Us*, loc. cit., p. 125.

[7] David Bohm, *The Special Theory of Relativity*. (New York: W. A. Benjamin, Inc., 1965), p. 196.

[8] *Ibid.*

[9] *Bla-ma dgongs-'dus*, vol. 9, p. 521.

[10] *Bla-ma yang-tig*, part I, p. 521.

[11] *Ibid.*, p. 513.

[12] *Ibid.*, pp. 513 f.

[13] It is significant that the Tibetan translation of the Indian word *buddha* (past participle of the verbal root *budh* "to wake up") is quite distinct from the connotation of the Indian word. This shows that the Tibetan translators were persons alive to their task and not mere robots randomly picking from the various entries in a dictionary (as is unfortunately done by a number of Western translators and their Eastern imitators).

[14] *Bla-ma yang-tig*, part I, p. 516.

[15] "a person who has found the answer to his problems" would be the closest rendering of this technical term.

[16] *Bla-ma yang-tig*, part I, p. 517.

[17] Or, as R. D. Laing, *The Politics of Experience* (New York: Ballantine Books, 1967), poignantly puts it: "What we most need is to be cured of our blasted normalcy" – normalcy being the split-up condition of the human psyche.

[18] Calvin O. Schrag, *Experience and Being* (Evanston: Northwestern University Press, 1965), p. 113.

[19] On these technical terms, see in particular the reference in *Kindly Bent to Ease Us*, Part One.

[20] Quoted in *Bla-ma dgongs-'dus*, vol. 9, p. 547.

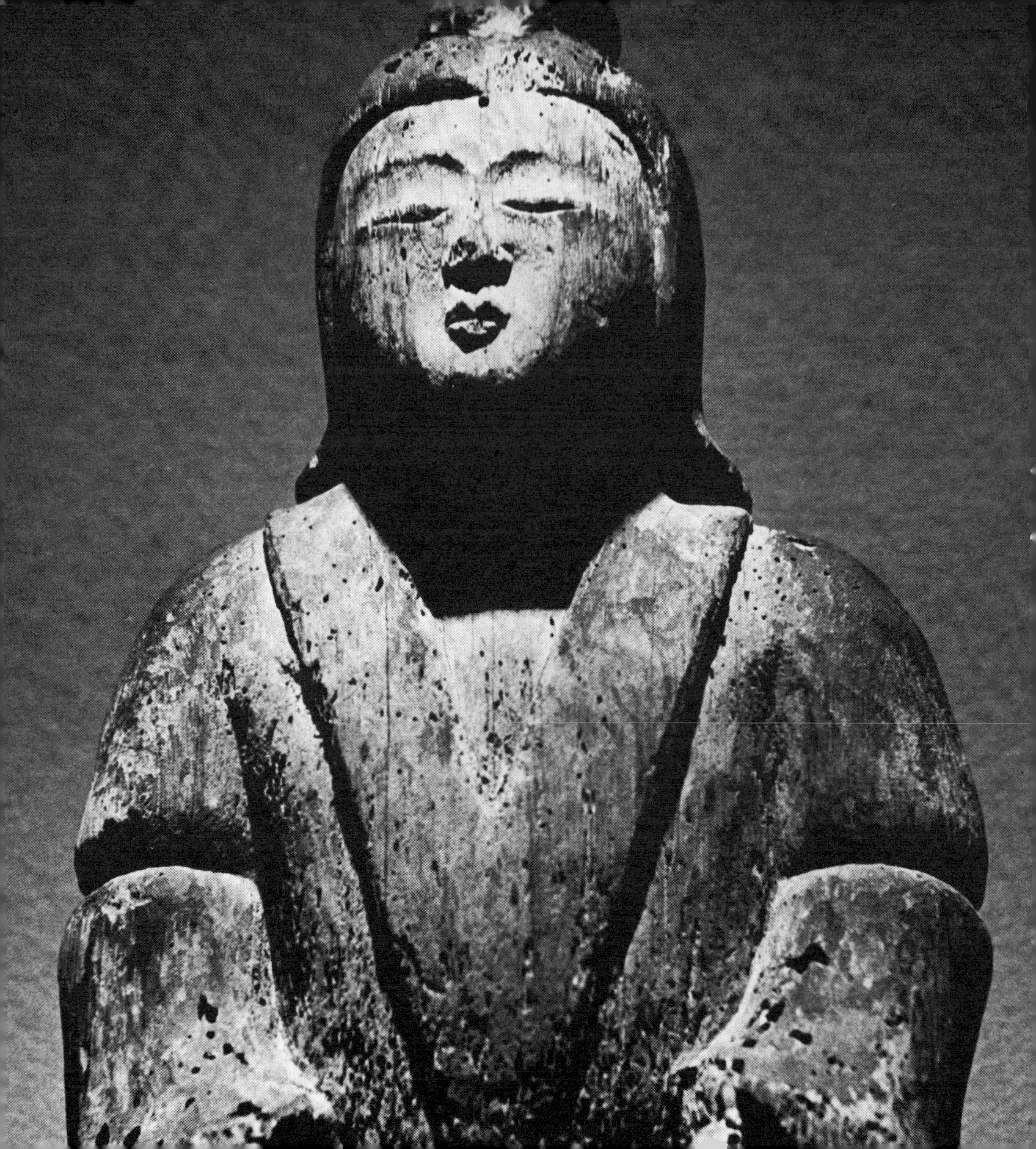

JEAN ERACLE

The Buddhist Way to Deliverance

Introduction

ALL the teaching given in India 2,500 years ago by the Buddha Sakyamuni can be summed up by the one word "Deliverance."

Deliverance is in fact the heart of the celebrated discourse at Benares on the Four Noble Truths, namely, the Noble Truth of Suffering, the Noble Truth of the Origin of Suffering, the Noble Truth of the Cessation of the Origin of Suffering, and the Noble Truth of the Way which leads to the Cessation of the Origin of Suffering.

The Four Noble Truths culminate in the third, Cessation.

The first two are a base, a starting point. In enunciating them the Buddha describes the condition of all of us. He shows us that if we are immersed in a great ocean of suffering, in the infinite cycle of birth and death, in massive sorrows and lamentations, it is due to our profound ignorance and to our passions. However, in compelling us to bear in mind the painful and transitory character of our existence, the Buddha does not wish to drive us to despair and force us to become still more gloomy and sad, but to make us understand that there exists a totally different posibility for us; this possibility, which is the aim of the third of the Four Noble Truths, is a state where ignorance and the passions are extinguished, a state in which all suffering is at an end, a state of perfect liberty, Deliverance, *Nirvana*. As the Buddha himself realised this state, he shows it to us, and in showing it to us, he indicates the way which permits us, in turn, to realize it.

This teaching is simple and defines the structure of all Buddhist doctrine. However, it does not include all its richness and all aspects of it.

Over more than forty years of preaching, Sakyamuni gave a vast and varied number of lessons, according to circumstances and the capacities and propensities of his listeners. The Buddha was a great, wise, and compassionate master. That is why he continually adapted his doctrine to the level of his disciples's understanding, giving to each what was suitable.

The Way of Deliverance, with its methodical stages and well devised order of practices, cannot be completely covered by one single discourse of Buddha.

The temptation into which students of Buddhism easily fall consists in regarding the Eightfold Path, as set forth in the discourse given at Benares or elsewhere, as expressing the complete way leading to Illumination. However, when all the scriptures are examined, it can be stated that the Buddha commended qualifications and practices not appearing in the text. It can also be stated that this path equals a certain degree of development and that it is not given in the same form and the same manner to everyone who aims at Deliverance.

Although it is impossible to expound all aspects of the teaching in a few pages, we are going to try to present the essence of the most important ways shown by the Master. To do this we shall not rely upon some particular discourse of the Buddha, but on the Scriptures as a whole, and on early commentators who completed a synthesis of the Doctrine in former times. Our account will necessarily remain concise, and we shall not be able to note divergences which appear here and there among commentators or the different traditions.

The Three Saints

Deliverance is not separable from *Bodhi*, that is to say, from Awakening, from Illumination. *Bodhi* is like the gateway to Deliverance. In fact it is due to it that the sage realizes he is completely delivered and consequently that there is nothing more of this aim to undertake.

Of what does *Bodhi* consist?

Vasubandhu answers this question in his *Abhidharmakośa* (VI, 67), an important work reflecting the different traditions of the ancient school of *Sarvāstivādin*. He says: "*Bodhi* is consciousness of the End (*Kshayajñāna*) together with consciousness of Non-Apparition (*Anutpādajñāna*) ... by means of these two ideas ignorance is completely renounced: from the first one indeed knows that the task is fulfilled; from the second it is known that the task will never be fulfilled."

Consciousness of the End is vivid proof that within oneself all streams of passion are cut off and, consequently, one is living one's last existence.

Consciousness of Non-Apparition, closely allied to consciousness of the End, is understanding that the stream of passions, being completely cut off, will never be born again, and that there is nothing more to do, neither to destroy them nor to prevent them re-appearing.

When taking into consideration the beings who attain it, this *Bodhi*, gateway to Deliverance, becomes threefold.

"*Bodhi*," writes Vasubandhu, "owing to the difference between the Saints who gain it, is three fold: there is the *Bodhi* of Disciples (*Śrāvakabodhi*), the *Bodhi* of Individual Buddhas (*Pratyekabuddhabodhi*) and the Supreme and Perfect *Bodhi* (*Anuttarasamyaksambodhi*)."

These three kinds of *Bodhi* are the result of three spiritual journeys, usually described as "Vehicles" (*Yāna*). The Bodhi of Disciples is the final fruit of merits acquired by the Vehicle of the Disciples (*Śrāvakayāna*); the *Bodhi* of the Individual Buddhas is the result of the Vehicle of the Individual Buddhas (*Pratyekabuddhayāna*); the Supreme and Perfect *Bodhi* is the attribute of the perfected Buddhas; it is the perfection obtained through the Vehicle of the Bodhisattvas (*Bodhisattvayāna*), also described by the term Great Vehicle (*Mahāyāna*).

These three Vehicles are known in all the ancient Buddhist schools. They are to be found in the teaching of the different schools of the olden branches of *Mahāsaṅghika* as well as in the holy books of the Sthavira branch derived from the vanished schools of *Sarvāstivādin*, or the still extant school of *Theravādin*. They are met with again in the immense literature of the Great Vehicle, the basis of the later schools of the same name. The three ways can therefore be thought of as belonging to the earliest teaching and as truly reflecting the Master's own ideas.

Simplified picture of ancient Buddhist Schools

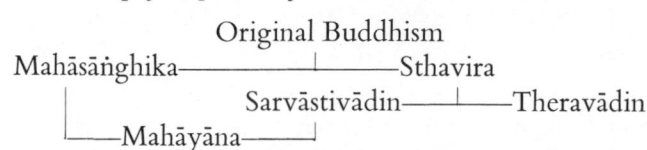

```
              Original Buddhism
Mahāsaṅghika─────────┴─────────Sthavira
                   Sarvāstivādin────┴────Theravādin
      └────Mahāyāna────┘
```

The three ways were debated endlessly in the ancient schools. It seems that, for them, the three Vehicles were distinct from one another, and it was possible to pass from one to the other only in the first stages. In later schools founded on the great *Mahāyāna Sūtras*, the first two Vehicles became provisional stages gradually leading beings, by moving more deeply inwards, towards the adoption of the third Vehicle, ending in the Supreme and Perfect Awakening. From this point of view it is called the Unique Vehicle (*Ekayāna*) of the Buddhas.

We are now going to explain the Three Vehicles in broad outline. To do this we shall draw principally on the teaching of the ancient schools and in particular on the tradition of *Sarvāstivādin* as found in the authoritative work of the great master Vasubandhu (IV century AD), the *Abhidharmakośa*, already quoted.

The Vehicle of the Disciples

According to Asaṅga, contemporary and brother of Vasubandhu, a Disciple is a person "diligent for his own liberation, with the aim of freeing himself by cultivating detachment" and who, "practising the major and minor virtues by training energy, puts an end to suffering" (*Abhidharmasamuccaya* II,3,1).

The objective of the Disciple's aim is clearly defined: the Disciple works hard for his own deliverance; and as he conceives deliverance as the absence of all desire, he takes the Vehicle for the cultivation of detachment. It is therefore in practicing all the virtues promoting complete detachment that he ends suffering.

How does the Disciple attain *Bodhi*?

By the help of what are called the thirty-seven Aids to Illumination (*Bodhipākṣikadharma*).

The thirty-seven Aids to Illumination are formed by seven groups of qualities that it is advisable to develop.

These groups are enumerated and explained at length in different passages in the Scriptures. For example, here is a statement of them which can be found in the celebrated canonical text of *Theravādin*, the *Mahāparinibbānasutta* (*Dīghanikāya*, II,119). In this text Buddha, who is on his way to the town where he will attain the Great Ultimate *Nirvana*, stops at Vaiśālī and gives the following instructions to his companions:

"Now, O Monks, you must grasp, follow, practice the doctrines which I have understood and taught, so that this religious life becomes permanent and lasting, to the greater advantage and good fortune of many, through compassion for the world and for its benefit, to the advantage and happiness of gods and men. And what are these doctrines which I have understood and taught that you should learn? They are the Four Applications of Attention, the Four Right Efforts, the Four Bases of Superior Powers, the Five Faculties, the Five Forces, the Seven Constituent Parts of Illumination and the Eight Constituent Parts of the Way."

Let us see in more detail of what each of the thirty-seven Aids to Illumination consists.

1. *The Four Applications of Attention* (*Smṛtyuoasthāna*)
There is a large number of texts enumerating and explaining the Four Applications of Attention. There are even *Sūtras* devoted to their explanation.

The Applications of Attention consist in maintaining attention on four objects: the body (*Kāya*), sensations (*Vedanā*), the mind (*Citta*) and the subjects of thought (*Dharma*).

This attention, called *Satipaṭṭhānasutta* (*Majjhimanikāya*, I,55), is present in him who devotes himself to it "only for knowledge, only for reflection and who remains free and unattached to anything in the world."

In this kind of exercise it is a matter simply of observing and seeing in order to ascertain what are all the phenomena which impose on our mind and senses and to understand the mechanism of their unfolding.

2. *The Four Right Efforts* (*Samyakprahāṇa*)
The Four Right Efforts, described in several passages in the Scriptures, concern good and bad thoughts and consequently the thoughts and bodily actions which follow from them.

Good thoughts promote spiritual progress: wisdom, peaceful contemplation, moral reflections, detachment, benevolence, etc.

Evil thoughts are those which inspire the three great impurities of error, desire, and anger and all the passions and defilement that proceed from them.

The first effort is to prevent (*Saṃvara*) the birth of evil thoughts.

The second effort is to dispel (*Prahāṇa*) evil thoughts when they are born.

The Three Vehicles of the Ancient Schools

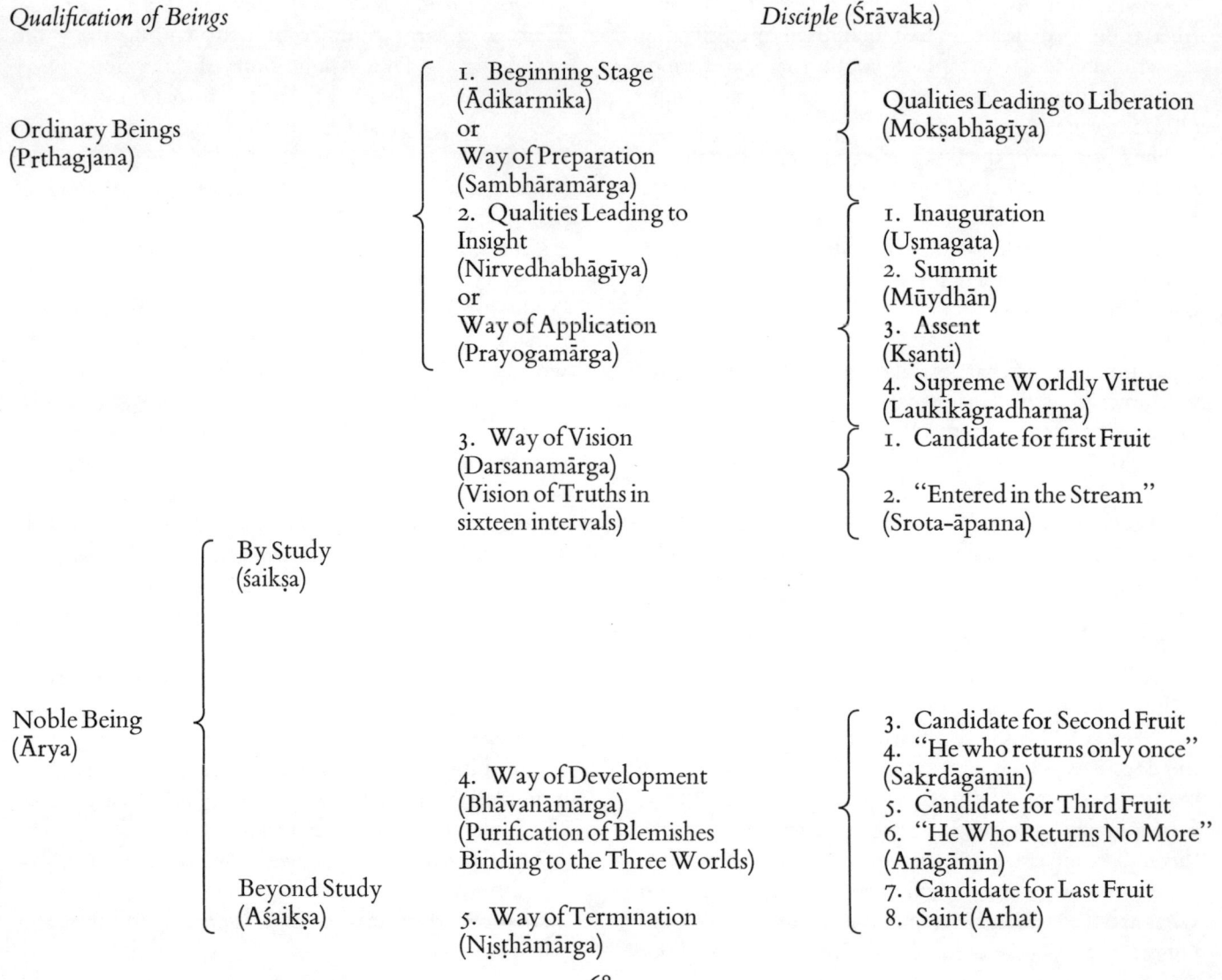

Qualification of Beings		Disciple (Śrāvaka)
Ordinary Beings (Pṛthagjana)	1. Beginning Stage (Ādikarmika) or Way of Preparation (Sambhāramārga)	Qualities Leading to Liberation (Mokṣabhāgīya)
	2. Qualities Leading to Insight (Nirvedhabhāgīya) or Way of Application (Prayogamārga)	1. Inauguration (Uṣmagata) 2. Summit (Mūydhān) 3. Assent (Kṣanti) 4. Supreme Worldly Virtue (Laukikāgradharma)
Noble Being (Ārya) — By Study (śaikṣa)	3. Way of Vision (Darsanamārga) (Vision of Truths in sixteen intervals)	1. Candidate for first Fruit 2. "Entered in the Stream" (Srota-āpanna)
Noble Being (Ārya) — Beyond Study (Aśaikṣa)	4. Way of Development (Bhāvanāmārga) (Purification of Blemishes Binding to the Three Worlds) 5. Way of Termination (Niṣṭhāmārga)	3. Candidate for Second Fruit 4. "He who returns only once" (Sakṛdāgāmin) 5. Candidate for Third Fruit 6. "He Who Returns No More" (Anāgāmin) 7. Candidate for Last Fruit 8. Saint (Arhat)

Individual Buddha (Pratyekabuddha)		*Bodhisattva*
	1. Preparatory phase (Course of Aspiration) (Adhimukticaryā)	
1–2. Long Preparation Lasting 100 Great Cosmic Periods (Mahākalpa) (1 and 2 take place in two different existences)	2. Phase of Resolution (Adhyāśayacaryā) beginning with The Vow of Bodhi (Praṇidhāna)	3. Countless periods (Asamkhyeya Kalpa) and 100 Cosmic Periods (Kalpa)
Eventually 3 and 4 (3–4)		
3 and 4. Last Existence in One Session and with Effort	3 and 4. Last Existence in One Session and *without Effort*	
8. Saint and Individual Buddha	8. Saint and Perfected Buddha (Samyaksambuddha)	

The third effort is to conjure up good thoughts (*Bhāvanā*).

The fourth effort is to protect (*Anurakṣaṇa*) good thoughts once they are born.

3. *The Four Bases of Superior Powers* (*Ṛddhipāda*)

The Superior Powers, which are the point of the following group, are well known to all the religious traditions of humanity, and particularly to the Indian. According to *Saṃyuttanikāya* (V, 275) they consist of being everywhere at once, in moving about without hindrance, for example, passing through walls, in entering the ground or emerging from it, walking on the waters, remaining seated in the air or in flying so far as to be able to touch the sun and the moon. Whatever interpretation be given to these marvellous feats, in Buddhist books they are regarded as the sign of the perfect control over his body which the saint acquires after practicing the Four Bases.

These are states of intense concentration (*Samādhi*), bringing together will (*Chanda*), energy (*Vīrya*), thought (*Citta*), and the spirit of enquiry (*Mīmāṃsā*).

In fact the Four Bases follow a perfectly logical order and symbolize a complete inner progress. If one concentrates will, one develops energy, which is the lasting activity of the will. If energy is concentrated, it is easy to control thought. And when thought is concentrated, it is capable of deep and meticulous enquiry.

4. *The Five Faculties* (*Indriya*)

The Five Faculties are spiritual qualities assisting man to develop his inner Deliverance. Therefore, they must not be confused with the six natural faculties formed of the five senses and the intellect.

The spiritual faculties are Faith (*Śraddhā*), Energy (*Vīrya*), Attention (*Smṛti*), Concentration (*Samādhi*), and Wisdom (*Prajñā*).

Faith is very clearly defined in the texts. The *Saṃyuttanikāya* (V, 196) says: "By the faculty of Faith the disciple is faithful: he has faith in the illumination of *Tathāgata*, the Blessed, the Saint, the Wholly Illuminated, He who is endowed with consciousness and prudence, the Blessed, the All-Knowing, the Supreme Guide for man's education, the instructor of gods and men, the Buddha, the Blissful."

Elsewhere Faith is called applying oneself to the Four Noble Truths or to the Three Jewels of Buddha, of the *Dharma* (Doctrine), of the *Saṅgha* (Monastic Order), as well as to the rules of morality (*Śīla*) revered by Noble Beings. In fact, all these aims intended for the faith of Disciples recall in one way or another the Illumination attained by Buddha.

When Faith takes root in the Illumination of Buddha, the disciple is certainly helped on towards Deliverance. Clearly, in this sense, his energy grows. When energy develops, the disciple directs his mind upon the aim sought after and gives his attention to it. When attention is maintained, the power of concentration increases. And when concentration is realized, wisdom is manifest.

As is seen, the faculty of Faith is the gateway to others. It shows its importance in Buddhist thought.

5. *The Five Forces* (*Bala*)

In their first phase the Five Faculties remain weak. They can therefore be thwarted by their opposites: doubt, torpor, inattention, scatteredness, and stupidity. However, as they are cultivated, they become stronger accordingly. When they become strong enough not to be thwarted any more, they become the Five Forces. The Five Forces correspond strictly to the Five Faculties. There is therefore the Force of Faith (*Śraddhābala*), the Force of Energy (*Vīryabala*), the Force of Attention (*Smṛtibala*), the Force of Concentration (*Samādhibala*), and the Force of Wisdom (*Prajñābala*).

6. *The Seven Constituent Parts of Illumination* (*Bodhyaṅga*)

The following group is made up of the Seven Constituent Parts of Illumination, customarily arranged in the order which follows: Attention (*Smṛti*), Scrutiny of Phenomena (*Dharmapravicaya*), Energy (*Vīrya*), Delight

(*Prīti*), Tranquillity (*Praśrabdhi*), Concentration (*Samādhi*), and Equanimity (*Upekṣā*).

The texts explaining this series define the first term as "the highest degree of skill in Attention"; due to this skill the disciple is capable of "wisely scrutinising all phenomena." Such an examination "starts Energy going" and from it "is born the delight in being free from everything sensual." Succeeding this delight "the body and the mind become tranquil." From this wholly relaxed and happy state, Concentration is born, from which comes Equanimity.

7. *The Eight Constituent Parts of the Way* (*Mārgāṅga*)
When the Buddha announced in the sermon at Benares that he had found The Middle Way, and when a little later he declared the last of the Four Noble Truths, he enumerated eight qualities. These eight qualities appear at the end of the list of the thirty-seven Aids to Illumination. They are: Right Seeing (*Samyagdṛṣṭi*), Right Purpose (*Samyaksaṃkalpa*), Right Speaking (*Samyagvāc*), Right Action (*Samyakkarmānta*), Right Means of Existence (*Samyagājīva*), Right Effort (*Samyagvyāyāma*), Right Attention (*Samyaksmṛti*), and Right Concentration (*Samyaksamādhi*).

Right Seeing is nothing less than understanding the Four Noble Truths.

Right Purpose consists in avoiding greedy, angry and wicked thoughts.

Right Speaking is free of deceit, slander, insult, and empty chattering.

Right Action requires abstention from taking the life of living beings, from taking what is not given, and from committing lewdness.

Right Means of Existence consists in adopting a kind of life or profession which does not involve infringing the principles expressed in the other constituent parts of the Way. The ideal means of existence is portrayed by the life of the mendicant monk, completely devoted to the spiritual search and to teaching the Doctrine.

Right Effort and Right Attention consist of the Four Efforts and the Four Applications of Attention which begin the series of thirty-seven Aids to Illumination.

As for Right or Perfect (*Samādhi*) Concentration it is described in the Scriptures as the development of four degrees of contemplation or *Dhyāna*.

These four degrees of contemplation are important throughout the Buddhist tradition. The *Saṃyuttanikāya* (V, 8) describes them thus:

"A monk freed from passions and evil thoughts attains the first *Dhyāna* full of delight and pleasure, and remains there; this *Dhyāna* is attended with reasoning and inquiry, and it is born of solitude.

"When, being in a state of inner serenity, the intellect fixed on a single point, reasoning and inquiry ceasing, the monk attains the second *Dhyāna*, filled with delight and pleasure, and remains there; this *Dhyāna* is born of concentration and is free of reasoning and inquiry.

"Even-minded, indifferent to joy, the monk remains in attention, master of himself: he then experiences in his body the pleasure which the Noble Beings call 'Living in Equanimity'; attentive and happy he reaches the third *Dhyana* and remains there.

"Dismissing pleasure and pain, indifferent to the disappearance of exaltation and to dejection, he attains the fourth *Dhyāna* and remains there; this *Dhyāna* is pleasureless and painless, through its purity of attention and equanimity. That, O Monks, is what is called Right Concentration."

★ ★ ★

When the thirty-seven Aids to Illumination are re-examined, it is immediately noticeable that a certain number of them are referred to several times.

For example, Attention first appears in the configuration of the Four Applications, then as one of the Five Faculties, as one of the Five Forces, as one of the Seven Constituent Parts of Illumination, and as one of the Eight Constituent Parts of the Way.

Energy first conceals itself under the appearance of the Four Efforts, to appear next among the Four Bases of Power, the Five Faculties and the Five Forces, in the Seven Constituent Parts of Illumination, and finally as the sixth part of the Way.

Concentration also appears several times: in the Five Faculties and the Five Forces, in the Seven Constituent Parts of Illumination, and as the last Constituent Part of the Way.

This had not been overlooked by the commentators of old, and Vasubandhu quotes a tradition which reduces the thirty-seven Aids to ten qualities only.

It is explained as follows: as Buddha showed, the thirty-seven qualities mentioned are in seven groups corresponding to different stages of the progress to *Bodhi*.

Vasubandhu, who meditates on the different interpretations current among the *Sarvāstivādin*, puts it this way in his *Abhidharmakośa* (VI, 70):

"The different Aids to Illumination form seven groups which are portioned out, in order, between the beginning stage, the qualities leading to Insight, Development and Vision.

In the beginning stage (*Ādikarmika*) are the Instructions for Attention, because at this phase the body is studied, etc.

In Inauguration (*Uṣmagata*) are Right Efforts, because in this stage energy increases, an increase which is the principle of progress.

In the Summit (*Mūrdhan*) are the Bases of Power, because due to them, it is made sure that the proper roots cannot be lost.

In Assent (*Kṣānti*) are the Faculties, because in this stage, Faith, Energy, etc., achieve sovereign quality from the fact that in Assent one is unlikely to fall again.

In Supreme Virtue (*Agradharma*) are the Forces, for in this stage, Faith, Energy, etc., can no longer be overwhelmed by the passions – the latter being of no further concern – or by other worldly occupations.

In the Way of Development (*Bhāvanāmārga*) are the Constituent Parts of Illumination because this way is on the verge of Illumination, that is, consciousness of Impoverishment and consciousness of Non-Appearance, from which the Way of Vision is separated by the Way of Development.

In the Way of Vision (*Darśanamārga*) there are the Constituent Parts of the Way, because this path is characterized by conduct: in fact, it proceeds quickly.

But, it will be said, the Way of Vision preceeds Development. Why not keep to the order? The *Sūtra* names the Constituent Parts of Illumination before, and those of the Noble Way after, so as to have an order corresponding to the number of Parts, first seven, then eight.

According to what has been said, it is evident that the ancient tradition upon which Vasubandhu pondered divided the Vehicle of the Disciples into four great stages:

First: The Beginning Stage;
Second: The Qualities leading to Insight;
Third: The Path of Vision;
Fourth: The Path of Development.

In his *Abhidharmasamuccaya* (I, 4) Asaṅga teaches a path of five stages: "The Noble Path," he says, "is fivefold: the Path of Preparation (*Sambhāramārga*), the Path of Application (*Prayogamārga*), The Path of Vision (*Darśanamārga*), the Path of Development (*Bhāvanāmārga*) and the Path of Termination (*Niṣṭhāmārga*)."

As further on (ibid) Asaṅga divides the Oath of Application into the four qualities leading to insight (*Nirvedhabhāgīya*), it can be seen that the order he gives is exactly the same as that given by Vasubandhu.

Vasubandhu's beginning stage corresponds to Asaṅga's Path of Preparation. Then, the next three stages follow the sequence common to both teachers. Asaṅga adds the Path of Termination to them. In fact, the last stage defines only the state of those who have come to the

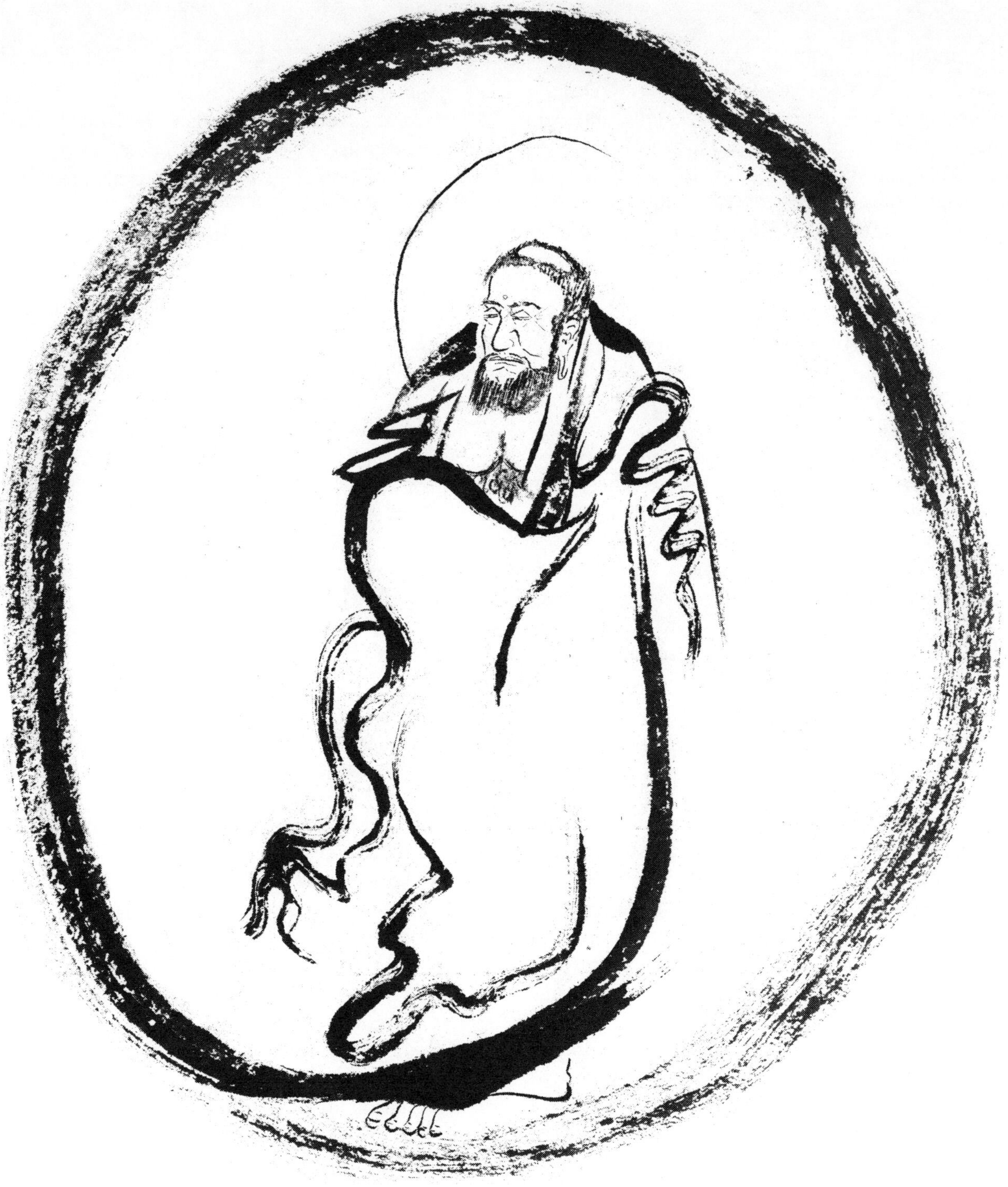

end of their spiritual search. At this stage the Disciple realizes ten qualities: he completely possesses the eight qualities conveyed in the Eight Constituent Parts of the Path; furthermore, he is adorned with Perfect Freedom (*Samyagvimukti*) and Perfect Consciousness of this Freedom (*Samyagjñāna*). The ten qualities are enumerated by Vasubandhu (*Abhidharmakośa*, VI, 75) in such a way that the two commentators are in agreement.

Several categories of beings correspond to these different stages. There are three categories with respect to development.

First of all there are ordinary beings (*Pṛthagjana*) and Noble Beings (*Ārya*).

In turn, Noble Beings are divided into two categories: one, those who are studying (*Śaikṣa*); the other, those who are no longer studying because they have gained the Ultimate Fruit, the State of Sainthood.

Ordinary beings, if they are on the way to Deliverance, belong to the beginning stage or are developing the qualities leading to insight.

It has been seen that beings of the first stage practice the Applications of Attention. In fact, they also practice all kinds of meritorious deeds called "Qualities leading to Freedom" (*Mokṣabhāgīya*), pertaining to body, speech, or to the mind.

"The quality leading to freedom," writes Vasubandhu (*Kośa*, VI, 25), "is essentially a mental act. But physical and vocal action are also qualities conducive to Freedom when they are surrounded with the resolve for Deliverance; resolution is a kind of conscious willing: in giving alms, a physical act, in undertaking to observe a rule, a vocal act, one forms a quality leading to Freedom when the strength of the desire for Deliverance qualifies these actions."

Beings of the second stage practice qualities leading to insight, with the fourth kind of Application of Attention. The thoughts to which they apply their attention are firstly aspects of the Four Noble Truths in relation to the Three Worlds of Desire, Form and the Formless, then of the Noble Truth of Pain in relation to the World of Desire solely (Vasubandhu, *Kośa* VI, 18–19).

Then these beings pledge themselves to the Path of Vision (*Darśanamārga*) and from this, become candidates for the Fruit of Admission to the Stream. They then acquire the dignity of Noble Being (*Ārya*).

The Path of Vision leads to the direct realization of the Four Noble Truths. It is a swift way because it is accomplished in sixteen intervals (Vasubandhu, *Kośa* VI, 26–28; Asaṅga, *Abhidarmasamuccaya*, I, 4).

These sixteen intervals, whose terms are quite difficult to grasp, amount, on the whole, to this:

1. Direct one's thoughts towards the Truth of Suffering in the World of Desire.
2. Perceive the Truth of Suffering in the World of Desire.
3. Direct one's thoughts towards the Truth of Suffering in the other two worlds.
4. Perceive the Truth of Suffering in the other two worlds.

These four intervals recur in relation to the other three Noble Truths.

By this method the shackles of the idea of a permanent self (*Satkāyadṛṣṭi*), of uncertainty (*Vicikitsā*), and of attachment to keeping rules and vows (*Śīlavratāparāmarśa*) are broken, and the First Fruit, Entrance into the Stream (*Srota-āpanna*), is gained.

The gaining of the First Fruit opens the entrance to the Path of Development (*Bhāvanāmārga*).

At the same time one becomes a candidate for the Second Fruit.

The Path of Development cleanses different kinds of impurities attaching to the Three Worlds, beginning with the coarsest, that is, those relating to the World of Desire.

By giving up the nine impurities bound to the World of Desire one becomes completely free of the first five shackles: the idea of a permanent self (*Satkāyadṛṣṭi*), uncertainty (*Vicikitsā*), attachment to keeping rules and vows (*Śīlavrataparāmarśa*), the lure of the World of Desire (*Kāmarāga*), and hostility (*Vyāpāda*). Attaining at the same time the Fruit of He who returns only once (*Sakṛdāgāmin*), one becomes a candidate for the Third Fruit and attains the state of He who returns no more (*Anāgāmin*).

In seeking to be free from the last five shackles – lure of the World of Form (*Rūparāga*), lure of the World without Form (*Ārūpyarāga*), pride (*Māna*), restlessness (*Auddhatya*) and ignorance (*Avidyā*) – while cleansing oneself from the nine blemishes which link with the two superior worlds, one becomes a candidate for the last Fruit.

When the latter is gained one becomes a Saint (*Arhat*). By the same fact one is settled in the Path of Termination and belongs to the category of those who are beyond the need to study (*Aśaikṣa*).

Such is the Vehicle of the Disciples.

The Vehicle of Individual Buddhas

Next to the Vehicle of the Disciples is the Vehicle of the Individual Buddhas.

In the *Abhidharmasamuccaya* (II, 3,1), Asaṅga describes the Individual Buddha as a person "bent on his own liberation, purporting to free himself by practising detachment, aiming to attain Illumination by proving the facts for himself," and, who "practicing the major and minor virtues by means of the cultivation of energy, whether or not having previously produced the qualities leading to insight, whether or not having previously obtained a Fruit, born in an epoch when there is no Buddha in the world, confronting the Noble Path by inner volition alone, remaining single like the horn of a rhinoceros or as an individual victor in a group, ends suffering."

On reading such a description, one is immediately struck by the close relationship uniting the Individual Buddha with the Disciple. In fact, like the latter, the man who pledges himself to the Path of Individual Buddhas has only one aim: his own liberation. Like the Disciple, he practices detachment and all the virtues for his personal deliverance. Moreover, the result of the two paths is similar: the Disciple and the Individual Buddha alone end suffering.

However, in several points, the Individual Buddha differs from the Disciple.

Whereas the Disciple advances only by basing himself on the teaching given by a Buddha, whether by listening to his oratory or by studying it while this teaching remains in the world, the Individual Buddha appears at a time when there is no Buddha in the world. The Individual Buddha, whether he lives by himself or in a group, must approach the Noble Path thinking about it for himself and by his own effort, "attaining Illumination by proving the facts for himself." On the other hand, while the Disciple can gain Deliverance either in the World of Desire or in the other two worlds, the Individual Buddha attains Illumination only in the World of Desire, during his final existence.

Vasubandhu (*Kośa*, II, 94) says this about the second Vehicle:

"There are two kinds of Buddhas: those who live together and those who resemble the horn of a rhinoceros.

"The first are former Disciples (*Śrāvaka*) who obtained the first or second Fruit of the Disciples under the sway of a Buddha.

"According to another view there are also ordinary beings who, in the Vehicle of the Disciples, have realized qualities leading to insight (*Nirvedhabhāgīya*). During a subsequent existence they realize the Path by themselves.

"The Individual Buddhas who resemble the horn of a rhinoceros live alone.

"He who resembles the horn of a rhinoceros prepares himself for Illumination over a hundred great cosmic periods of time. He obtains Illumination without the help of a teaching or of a revelation, by himself.

"The Individual Buddha is so called because he effects his own salvation without converting others."

The course of the Individual Buddha is summed up well in this short passage.

While still an ordinary being (*Pṛthagjana*), the candidate must first produce qualities leading to Liberation (*Mokṣabhāgīya*), then qualities leading to insight (*Nirvedhabhāgīya*). In other words, he follows the Path of Preparation and the Path of Application exactly as the Disciples. He can even gain the Fruit of Entry in the Stream (*Strota-āpanna*) by following the Path of Vision and gain the Fruit of He who returns only once (*Sakṛdāgāmin*) by cleansing himself from the principle impurities of the World of Desire on the Path of Development. As the Illumination of the Individual Buddhas is gained only in the World of Desire, the candidate must not obtain the third Fruit, for then he could not return to the world as an Individual Buddha.

The development of an Individual Buddha requires at least three existences.

In the first the candidate brings forth qualities leading to Liberation. In the second he practices talents leading to insight and, in due course, obtains the first and second Fruits. Finally, in the third, he covers all the remaining way to Illumination in one period and by intense effort. (*Kośa*, VI, 24).

It seems that the Individual Buddha who resembles the horn of a rhinoceros may have a longer course than that of Individual Buddhas living together. In fact he prepares himself in a hundred great cosmic periods for the attainment of Illumination (*Kośa*, III, 94).

Such is the Way of Individual Buddhas.

The Vehicle of Bodhisattvas

Asaṅga (*Abhidharmasamuccaya*, II, 3, 1) defines the adept of the Vehicle of Bodhisattvas as "a person devoted to the liberation of all beings, having the purpose of reaching Impermanent Nirvana" and who, "practicing the major and minor virtues by the training of energy, brings beings to maturity, cultivates the pure ground of Buddhas, receives prophecy, and attains the Perfect Awakening."

If this definition is compared with those of the first two Vehicles, it will immediately be recognized that the Bodhisattva is distinctly different from the Disciples and the Individual Buddhas.

His aim is different: he does not seek his own liberation, but the liberation of all beings; he does not aim to end suffering by attaining Perfect Nirvana, but aspires to Impermanent Nirvana.

Impermanent Nirvana is an important idea. Asaṅga (*idem*, II, 1,3) defines it as "Supreme Discontinuance." He says: "It is the Discontinuance of Buddhas and Bodhisattvas, and it is called Impermanent Nirvana because it is founded on their determination to give comfort and good fortune to all living beings."

In other words, while the Disciples and Individual Buddhas aspire to hurry away from this world's conflagration, the Bodhisattva seeks to remain here in order to help all those who are suffering. Consequently, while the Vehicle of Disciples and the Vehicle of Individual Buddhas emphasize complete detachment and the extinction of passions, the Bodhisattvas show compassion and love in remaining with beings in order to save them. Because there is a different point of view there is a different way.

According to Vasubandhu (*Kośa*, II, 44), who relates how the *Sarvāstivādin* see it, the Bodhisattva remains an ordinary man (*Pṛthagjana*) up to the moment when he manifests as a fully-fledged Buddha. During innumerable existences amongst beings, keeping clear of the

Paths of Vision and of Development, he accumulates all kinds of knowledge and merits which will bring beings to maturity and cause them to flower into Supreme and Perfect Illumination. In fact, the Bodhisattva, after long preparation, covers, during his last existence and just before *Bodhi*, the sixteen intervals of the Path of Vision, and the eighteen intervals of the Path of Development, in a single period and without any effort. At the same time, still without effort, he acquires all the talents and all the powers of a fully-fledged Buddha.

Properly speaking, the course of Bodhisattvas begins when they pronounce the great resolve (*Praṇidhāna*) to attain Supreme Illumination for the salvation of all beings.

"The vow of the Bodhisattva," writes Vasubandhu (*Kośa*, III, 96), "is to become a Buddha protecting the unprotected in a blind and unprotected world."

It is by virtue of such a vow, many times renewed, that Bodhisattvas prepare for Illumination during three countless cosmic periods.

"Why," asks the same scholar (*idem*, III, 93–94), "do the Bodhisattvas take so long a time to obtain Supreme Illumination once they have resolved to attain it?"

The answer is full of meaning.

"Because Supreme Illumination is very difficult to gain; it requires a vast accumulation of knowledge and merit, innumerable heroic deeds throughout three countless cosmic periods. It would be understandable that the Bodhisattvas sought this illumination which is so difficult to obtain if it were the only means of reaching Deliverance, but such is not the case. Why, therefore, do they undertake this infinite toil? For the good of others, because they wish to be capable of redeeming others from the great river of suffering. But what personal good do they find in the good of others? The good of others is their own good because they desire it. Who could believe you? Truly, men destitute of pity who think only of themselves have difficulty in believing in the altruism of Bodhisattvas; but compassionate men find it easy to believe. Do we not see men who are chronically lacking in pity finding pleasure in the suffering of others, even when it is of no advantage to them? Likewise must it be acknowledged that Bodhisattvas with their strong sense of pity find pleasure in doing good to others, without self-interest."

As the three countless periods are remarkable for compassion, they are equally so for the veneration of innumerable Buddhas, as the course of the future Buddha Sakyamuni shows:

"How many Buddhas," asks Vasubandhu (*Kośa*, IV, 110), "did the Blessed One venerate when he was a Bodhisattva? In the first countless period he venerated 75,000 Buddhas, in the second, 76,000, and in the third, 77,000."

The long process of becoming a mature Bodhisattva is also derived from the six great perfections called "*Pāramitā*."

How does the Bodhisattva fulfill each Pāramitā?

He fulfills the Gift (*Dāna*) by giving everyone everything, out of pity: when, from pity, without wishing for bliss, he gives everything to everyone, his eyes and the marrow in his bones, he fulfills the virtue of the Gift.

When, although he may not be detached, he does not become at all angry even though he breaks a limb, he then serves the virtues of Morality (*Śīla*) and Patience (*Kṣānti*).

Energy (*Vīrya*) in praise of Puṣya. When the Blessed One was a Bodhisattva, he saw the Tathāgata Puṣya making himself incandescent inside a mountain cave. He praised him for seven days and seven nights while standing on one foot.

Contemplation (*Dhyāna*) and Wisdom (*Prajñā*) immediately before Illumination. At the moment of the Diamond *Samādhi*, immediately before Illumination he fulfills the virtues of Contemplation and Wisdom (*Kośa*, IV, 112).

At the end of the second period the Blessed One won assurance of becoming Buddha on hearing the prediction which the Buddha Dīpaṅkara made to him. This assurance which makes a Bodhisattva an "unwavering" being (*Avaivartika*) opens the third period.[1]

Finally, when the three periods have elapsed, in the course of a hundred supplementary cosmic periods the aspirant behaves in a way which renders him worthy of obtaining all the characteristics of Buddhas, bearing the thirty-two marks of the Great Man (*Mahāpuruṣa*) and the eighty signs of beauty (*Kośa*, IV, 108).

Such is the course of Bodhisattvas according to the *Sarvāstivādin*.

The chief point of this method is to be found in the writings of other ancient schools.

In the *Mahāsaṅghika* (*Mahāvastu*, I, 46–63) the course comprises four great epochs: first there is the "natural" course (*Prakṛticaryā*), which corresponds to the Beginning Stage or Preparatory Path. During this period, the Bodhisattvas fulfills every kind of natural, meritorious action: respect for father and mother, homage to wise men, honesty, generosity towards others, worship of Buddhas.

At a certain moment they resolve to gain illumination. The stage at which they make this vow is the Course of Resolution (*Praṇidhānacaryā*).

They then devote themselves to the practices which lead to Awakening and are therefore in the period of Conformity (*Anulomacaryā*). They practice the Six *Pāramitā* which are the same as those of the Sarvāstivādin (*Mahāvastu*, III, 226, 2).

Finally they obtain prophecy and enter the Unwavering Course (*Avivartacaryā*).

According to the *Mahāsaṅghika* (*Mahāvastu*, I, 76), from their resolution Bodhisattvas pass through ten stages (*Bhūmi*), the last of which, Consecration (*Abhiṣeka*), is gained just before Illumination.

This course is to be found in the *Theravādin*, in particular in the *Mahāvaṃsa*, which describes the progress of the future *Sakyamuni*. This long poem tells how the Buddha for 100,000 cosmic periods uttered his vows before the Buddha Dīpaṅkara and received prophecy from him. From that moment he practiced ten Perfections (pali: *Pārami*): the Gift (p. *Dāna*), Honesty (p. *Sīla*), Renunciation (p. *Nekkhamma*), Wisdom (p. *Paññā*), Energy (p. *Viriya*), Patience (p. *Khanti*), Truth (p. *Sacca*), Resolution (p. *Adhiṭṭhāna*), Friendship (p. *Mettā*) and Equanimity (p. *Upekkhā*). (*Mahāvaṃsa*, st. 12–197).

The tradition of the *Theravādin* differs in more than one respect from other ancient schools. It places Dīpaṅkara in a far more distant epoch and has a different list of Perfections. However, it can be said that that the *Theravadin* agrees, in the main, with other schools.

The *Mahāyāna* books and their commentators are largely concerned with the Vehicle of the Bodhisattvas. The well-known events of the ancient schools are to be found in them: the Preparatory Period, the Noble Vow inaugurating progress in the *Pāramitā*, the Unwavering Stage. The six *Pāramitā* are those already known to the *Sarvāstivādin* and the *Mahāsaṅghika*, plus Means (*Upāya*), Vigor (*Bala*), Resolution (*Praṇidhāna*) and Consciousness (*Jñāna*). The ten Perfections are related to the ten stages (*Bhūmi*) whose poetic names differ from those in the *Mahāvastu*. The books of the Great Vehicle give importance to a particular state of mind called "Conception of Illumination" (*Bodhicitta*), a kind of seed, sown in the heart from seeing a Buddha, opening out through the Great Vows, and blooming at the moment of Supreme Awakening.

As there are many different interpretations and great details in the vast *Mahāyāna* literature, we cannot linger on them. We have given enough information to make the Vehicle of the Bodhisattvas understandable in its broad outline.

Conclusion

On perusing the three ways to Deliverance taught by the Buddha, one is struck by the inner logic which sustains them.

Throughout the different stages of which they are composed, each virtue to be developed, each practice to be implemented, and each obstacle to be warded off is precisely described.

Thus, the Master's teaching is like a great strategist's plan of battle. Knowing the positions of the enemy, the particular nature of the ground, as well as the qualities and defects of the three categories of combatants, the Buddha sets forth a detailed and extremely wise order of contest, such that he who pledges himself to follow it is sure of triumphing over ignorance and the passions, and thus of attaining the unalterable peace of Deliverance.

---

[1] There is doubt about the exact moment when the Unwavering State is gained. The *Kośa* seems to place it at the beginning of the hundred periods when the tokens appear. Other sources indicate the third period, as in Nāgārjuna's summary of the doctrine of *Sarvāstivādin*. See Conze E, *Buddhist Scriptures*. (Penguin Books, 1960), pp 30–33.

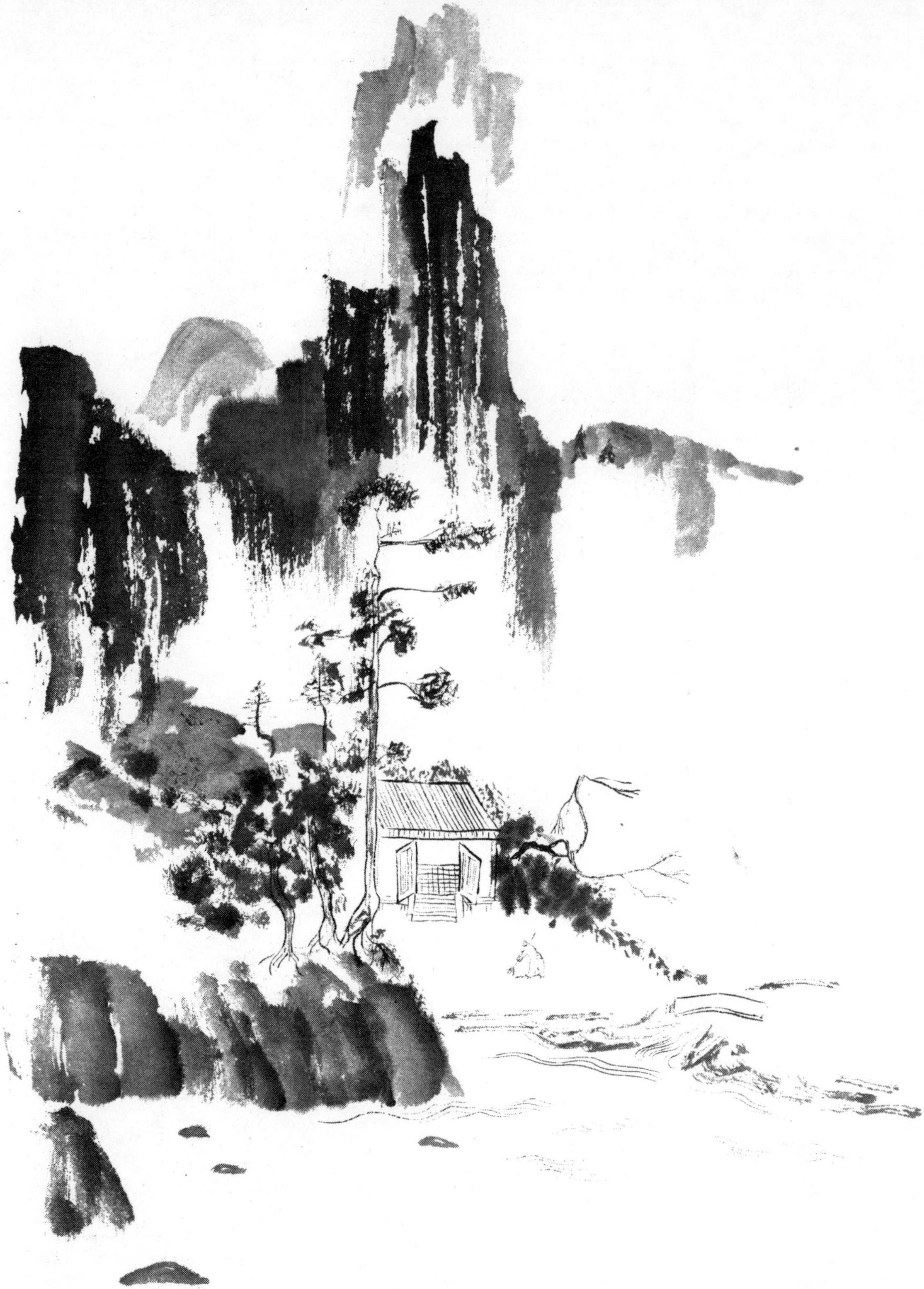

JOHN BLOFELD

Return to the Source
AN EXALTED FORM OF TAOIST MYSTICISM

TAOISM is a name covering widely different activities, but all based on the same fundamental understanding of the universe. Its multiform and colorful sects share similar concepts of the nature of the Tao and of its activity through cyclical change and the interaction of *yin* and *yang*. Yet so diverse are the applications of those concepts that almost anything one says about Taoism will be true only of some Taoists. Though the oldest form of Chinese mysticism, it is less widely known that Mahayana Buddhism, and some comparison between them may be a good way of introducing the subject.

A Comparison of Taoist and Buddhist Mysticism

The supreme mystical experience called by some Taoists "Return to the Source" is surely identical with what Mahayana Buddhists understand by Enlightenment and probably not different in kind from the experience known to Christian mystics as "Union with the Godhead." Its attainment requires restraint in conduct, transmutation of the baser passions and rigorous training in yogic contemplation leading to progressively expanding states of consciousness. The Taoist approach nevertheless differs from that of Mahayana Buddhists; for apart from differences of yogic method, some of which may be mere differences of terminology or of concept prior to realization, Taoist mystics do not feel the same compulsion as Mahayana Buddhists to attain the goal swiftly for the sake of all sentient beings. Less convinced than Buddhists of the reality of transmigration, what they seek to avoid is not the endless round of rebirth, but gradual disintegration leading to extinction.

As is now widely known, Mahayanists take a moralistic approach to the supreme attainment envisaged by both faiths, believing that sentient beings, as a result of primordial ignorance, are doomed to wander aeon upon aeon from life to life, all these lives being characterized by varying degrees of unsatisfactoriness (boredom, frustration, disappointment, bereavement, tension, pain, etc., etc.), from which there is no deliverance except through the cultivation of wisdom and compassion so as to achieve Enlightenment, of which the immediate fruit is liberation. Moreover, they conceive it their compassionate duty to attain Enlightenment as soon as possible, having previously vowed to remain within the round of birth and death as Bodhisattvas, that is to say, spiritual beings able to lead others towards liberation. Their compassion lends a terrible urgency to the task, all the more so as the sutras teach that unless great progress is made in this very life, it may be that many aeons must pass before another opportunity offers itself for one to take human birth, let alone be reborn in a land where the Doctrine of the Buddha is proclaimed. Both among Chinese and Tibetan Buddhists, compassion is the main urge towards winning Enlightenment. Taoists, though by no means lacking in compassion, feel a different urge.

Generally speaking, Taoists are much less convinced of the inevitability of rebirth within the well-nigh perpetual round of transmigration. Many are agnostics, apt to reflect that no one knows for certain whether or not such a round exists, whether death is the end of a person's existence, or whether it leads – if anywhere – to a state better or worse than the present life. Many others believe that at death one's twin souls separate, the one to rise to a higher sphere, the other to descend to a lower; but that, except in special circumstances, both will thereafter sooner or later disintegrate, so that immortality is not a universal condition but one that must be cultivated. That being so, the worst to be feared is total disintegration, if not at the time of death then subsequently. Such a prospect is less daunting than the prospect of aeon upon aeon of existence inseparable from suffering; and it does not give rise to an urge to rescue countless other sentient beings from that fate. It would, I rather think, be fair to say that to the majority of Taoists immortality in one form or another (and many forms have been conceived) is not the lot of all, but only of those who carefully "cultivate the Way." It is desirable and well worth winning, but the alternative – disintegration – is not likely to seem terrifying or even utterly unwelcome to one who has thoroughly enjoyed a life lived according to Taoist principles.

Basic Concepts of Taoism

Before describing the means employed to attain exalted mystical experience, I shall very briefly set forth some of the basic concepts common to most Taoists. Now that the communists have swept away all outward vestiges of Taoism on the Chinese mainland, the past tense may be more appropriate than the present, but for convenience sake I shall generally use the latter. Taoism is a way of life, a philosophy and (for many of its adherents) a religion as well. No one knows when it began, for the writings of Lao-tzû and of Confucius, both of whom lived some two and a half millenia ago, indicate that some of its concepts and manifestations had long existed when they wrote. Traditionally, the Founder was the Yellow Emperor (accession 2697 B.C.), but scholars would laugh at me if I presumed to accept that tradition. During the last two thousand years (and some say for even longer), Taoism and Buddhism have interacted upon each other in China – when and to what degree is of historical interest but not of great importance to students of mysticism, who judge the methods employed for mystical attainment by their effectiveness, not by their labels. Ultimate Truth, however many its facets at the lower levels of perception, is what is; there cannot be several of them, only different names, concepts and methods of attaining it.

The Tao The Tao (a literal translation of this term is "Way") is unknowable, being beyond the power of words to convey (without diminishing its sublimity) and of thought to conceive; but mystics hold that it can be sensed by direct intuition. It has been apprehended as having two aspects. As the progenitrix of existence, it is a sublime, quiescent, limitless void, spotless in its purity, the wellspring and container of the myriad forms; yet, simultaneously, it *is* the myriad forms, the "stuff" or "substance" of their being. Void, it is also non-void; of a seemless unity, it is also multiform; the container of the universe, it is also the contained! Logically, this is nonsense; intuitively, it has been apprehended thus by mystics of all faiths and there have even been distinguished modern physicists whose thoughts have been impelled in this direction. The concept exactly conforms with what Mahayana Buddhists term the absolute (void) and relative (non-void) aspects of truth or reality. One cannot convince sceptics of the rightness of this concept, for they will be unwilling to undergo the arduous training required for direct perception; but it is possible to convince oneself – first by reflecting that it is extremely unlikely that madmen living at different ages in different continents would all dream the same dream, from which it follows that mystics cannot be thus regarded; eventually, by perceiving the truth intuitively as a result of properly directed yogic endeavor. There are expanded states of consciousness in which the seemingly giant paradox is discovered to be an obvious truism, and one laughs with joy at finding the hitherto puzzling reality so utterly simple. Alas, that does not mean one can then convey it convincingly to another person in a few well-chosen words. *Quite* on the contrary!

Cyclic Change The Tao is eternal and changeless; yet the myriad forms (also the Tao) are subject to unceasing change. Change proceeds in cycles which operate on macrocosm and microcosm identically. These cycles, being vast, manifold, and closely interwoven are difficult to isolate or comprehend; yet some of their effects, such as the movements of heavenly bodies and the progress of the seasons, are readily apparent; by studying the cycles profoundly, one can to some extent anticipate the future and foresee the consequences of particular lines of action. Better still, such study leads to a state of tranquil acceptance of all life's ups and downs; serenity in the face of gain and loss, rising and falling, life and death, is the beginning of true wisdom and a source of unrivalled happiness.

Yin and Yang The myriad forms are forever coming into existence, waxing, waning, and dissolving or being transmuted one into another. When they newly arise, the Tao is not thereby augmented; when they dissolve, the Tao is not thereby diminished; they *are* the Tao; as one comes, another goes and *vice versa*. That these forms differ in so many ways one from another is due to the interaction of two perpetually interweaving principles – *yin* and *yang*, the one dark, negative, passive, etc.; the other light, positive, active, etc. These two are equally essential to the existence of any form whatsoever, neither being superior to, or more desirable than, the other. Since each contains the seed of its own opposite, "pure *yin*" or "pure *yang*" is unthinkable. Taoists bestow on the interaction of *yin* and *yang* the same careful attention that they give to the cycles of change, for the two are intimately bound up with each other and studying them is a source of profound knowledge about "the way things go" in every sphere ranging, say, from chemistry to statecraft.

The "Supernatural" To a Taoist, the notion that anything can be supernatural is patently absurd, for what could lie above, beyond, or below the infinite Tao?; and what is Nature but the Tao? Yet there are Taoists who believe in many things that *we* may call supernatural. There is of course absolutely no concept of a creator-god, of a deity standing apart from creation (and therefore separate from the Tao); Taoism and Buddhism are at one on this fundamental point. However, as with many Buddhists, this does not prevent Taoists from believing in the existence of teeming orders of beings invisible to man and with varying characteristics different in some respects from those of men and animals. Where Taoist agnostics give little or no thought to this matter, and a good many others deem it wise to treat such beings respectfully but keep them at a safe distance, there are plenty of Taoists who seek to establish various kinds of relationship with divine and demonic orders. The pantheon of *popular* Taoism teems with gods, planetary divinities, deified humans, and immortals, and there is a lively belief in ghosts and many kinds of demons; but such beliefs are by no means an essential part of Taoism, which enjoins no fixed articles of belief whatsoever. It is obvious to every thinking man that there are all sorts of benign and malignant forces at work in the universe; but whether one personifies them in the form of gods and demons, conceives of them as light and dark forces of a much more subtle nature, or accounts for their operation in terms of "luck," pathologic conditions of mind, or whatever, is entirely a matter of personal choice. Thus a Westerner who desires to attain sublime states of consciousness and ultimately the highest mystical goal by Taoist means is not in the least obliged to take up the beliefs or practices of what may be called popular Taoism, interesting and at times rewarding as some of them may be. Even among Chinese Taoists, though many set great store by what we should call spiritual healing, exorcism, divination and so on, there are others who smile at such practices, holding them to be at best fascinating by-paths leading away from the ardent quest of the true mystic.

The Influence of Buddhism

That in China Buddhism and Taoism influenced each other at the later stages is not to be doubted. Ch'an (Zen) in particular is a product of a happy marriage between the two systems; and the kind of high mysticism which forms the main subject of this article is probably another offspring of that marriage. On the other hand, I do not find myself in ready agreement with those scholars who, perceiving close similarities between Taoist yoga and such Hindu-Buddhist yogas as *kundalini*, *tumo* and *powa*, as well as the identity of the Taoist *ch'i* (vital energy) with the Indian *prana*, affirm that Buddhism must have influenced Taoism at least two centuries before the beginning of the Christian era. If the goal of high mysticism and the means by which men seek to attain it are real, just as, say, cooking is real, one can suppose that they have several times been independently discovered, as was probably the case with the arts of starting a fire and cooking food. This is not perhaps of much consequence, one way or the other, but, in the absence of clear evidence, to claim that Taoist yoga must undoubtedly be an offspring of Buddhist yoga is to diminish the value of both by suggesting that they do not have the validity of "real things" discoverable by all.

Varied Applications of Taoist Concepts

Historically, the concept that all processes whatsoever in the universe occur in accordance with the same cycles of change, whether at the macrocosmic or microcosmic level, has led to a very strange phenomenon, namely that Taoist manuals setting forth applications of knowledge of the cycles are used as guides to an astonishingly wide range of subjects. Thus, the same text may be used for such diverse purposes as learning to live in harmony with nature's rhythms, teaching a prince how best to govern his state, planning military strategy, performing life-prolonging seminal-retention yogas, creating miniature landscapes, practising defensive combat, playing *wei ch'i* (a kind of chess known in Japanese as *go*), performing alchemical experiments, etc., etc., etc. It is as though one were to use a work of Plato, Malthus, Marx or Einstein as a guide to statecraft, strategic warfare, bed-chamber arts, and experiments in chemistry with the same hope of success! That such a thing was possible in China was partly due to the very special nature of the Chinese written language, which allows phrases to carry numerous meanings, and partly to Taoist insistence that there is nothing in the universe that does not proceed in accordance with regular and uniform cyclic change. In a way, the result has been unfortunate, for it makes many Taoist works exceedingly difficult to translate and by no means easy to understand. The difficulty is compounded by the deliberate choice of esoteric language to guard Taoist mysteries from the eyes of the profane – a necessary precaution, as many yogic practices are dangerous to oneself and others if performed without proper oral instruction. Naturally these enigmatic manuals fell into the hands of Taoists of varying spiritual and mental caliber, and this may have resulted in their being used for purposes very different from the range of purposes intended by the writers.

Among the applications of Taoist principles to specific activities that were to be found in various Taoist hermitages up to the communist take-over in the middle of this century were the following:

Quietistic living Some recluses sought to live in harmony with nature's rhythms without reference to the possibility of there being existence in some form beyond the grave or to any specifically religious notion. They desired to be healthy, happy, long-lived, and serene, enjoying moonlight, the plash of falling water, the beauty of trees, flowers and curious rock-formations or mountain scenery, sunshine but also snowfall, rain and thunder, without the smallest hankering for wealth, status, luxury, honor, life-after-death, or any of goals pursued in the "world of dust" beyond the hermitage's walls.

Mastery of nature's secrets The purpose was, in its way, scientific, the knowledge of nature's specific workings being applied to such pursuits as healing (both herbal and spiritual), exorcism, gardening, and alchemy, the object of this last being the compounding of an elixir able to prolong life and cure every kind of ill and/or transmuting base metals into gold.

Prolongation of life and retention of youthful vigor These were attempted, sometimes with obvious success, by a variety of means including meditation, yogic and calisthenic exercises, following particular health regimes and spending much time in the open air while gardening, planting, culling mountain herbs, and so on.

Intercourse with invisible orders of beings This activity was very often the means by which the hermits secured enough income to supply their slender needs, as the peasants who visited the hermitages, especially on festival days, expected to attend rituals pleasing to the gods and were by no means averse to having the local ghosts and demons satisfactorily subjugated. (It is impossible to say what proportion of the recluses had faith in the value of their rites as opposed to regarding them as a tiresomely necessary source of income.)

The search for immortality The several kinds of immortality envisaged by different sects or communities of Taoists included: "transmogrification," or transmuting one's physical body into a "jadelike" (etherial) substance impervious to heat, cold, hunger, thirst, and the laws of gravity. Those who succeeded were said to go away, sometimes leaving their garments behind as a sign, to join their fellow immortals in palaces of cloud or fairy realms and dwell in blissful tranquility for centuries, if not forever. Another kind was "generation of an immortal foetus" by strenuous yogic means, that is to say creating a spiritual body able to go forth from the physical body at times, perhaps to multiply itself into several according to need, and to survive physical dissolution. There was also refinement of one's upper soul or integration of the upper and lower souls, so as to win spiritual immortality after death; and refinement of one's principle of consciousness so as to achieve rebirth under auspicious conditions (possibly a notion borrowed from Buddhism).

Achieving the supreme mystical goal This was the chief concern of the most spiritually advanced Taoists and the one with which the rest of this article is concerned. It is, I believe, a close equivalent of the Buddhist quest for Enlightenment, but Enlightenment as envisaged by Theravadin rather than Mahayana Buddhists, since there is no sense of obligation to achieve it out of compassionate concern for others. It was seldom called Enlightenment; of the various names used for it, I liked "Return to the Source," in the sense of being merged indivisibly with the Tao. Despite the similarity to the Buddhist approach both in concept and, with a few minor differences, in method, it may appeal to those Westerners who, while already convinced of the possibility of undergoing this supreme experience, find it hard to accept the Buddhist doctrine regarding the cycle of rebirth, or who prefer to pursue the goal apart from any overtly religious context (except insofar as this quest in itself is perhaps the very highest form of religion). The methods used involve a particular mode of life (preferably *but not necessarily* lived in a small community somewhere remote from worldly life and close to nature), cultivating a particular attitude of mind and performing yogas ranging from those involving various physical practices to pure contemplative yoga.

Cultivating the Way

Introductory We now approach an exalted subject, for the task to be achieved is nothing less than cultivation of body and mind so as to attain progressively expanded states of consciousness that will culminate in the sublime experience of coming face to face with reality itself! This is the very acme of human endeavor; all other tasks pale in its effulgent light; world conquerors such as Alexander or Napoleon become puny men in comparison with the world-transcending adepts who achieve this high goal. Needless to say, it is not easily achieved and the number of successful adepts (though for obvious reasons this remains unknown since a realized adept *never* speaks of his supreme achievement) can scarcely be great! Yet the attempt is well worthwhile; even very modest success will contribute to improved health, the prolongation of youthful vigor for those who embark upon it early, the likelihood of an increased lifespan and, above all, the attainment of a joyous tranquility that will make the adept immune to fate's cruelest arrows and able to face even death with smiling imperturbability! At least, these are some of the minor fruits that Taoists claim for the practice, and I have met recluses whose speech, conduct, and appearance strongly support that claim.

Alas, I am far from being competant to give full instructions for achieving successful cultivation. For this, an excellent teacher is required; all I can do is to give a general outline of the kind of practices that, taken all together, comprise what is known as Cultivation of the Way or Seeking to Return to the Source. During the long and happy years I spent in China, visiting many of its innumerable sacred mountains, my chief interest was Buddhism; so, though I stayed in many Taoist hermitages for varying lengths of time, I did not undergo prolonged training under a Taoist teacher; whatever I know about mystical yogic contemplation is principally derived from Chinese and Tibetan Buddhist teachers, and it is with some temerity that I write specifically on Taoist cultivation. On the other hand, I have discovered that very few English-speaking people (whether Western or Chinese) spent much time in Taoist hermitages during the last phase of their existence in mainland China; and that those who did happen to visit one or two usually did so merely for the convenience of having a nice place to stay in spectacularly beautiful natural surroundings. I did at least eagerly question the recluses I met on many aspects of their beliefs and practices; so, without being at all well-qualified to write of what they did to cultivate the Way, I am perhaps less ill-qualified than most people to give some account of it in English. Some of what follows may seem rather irrelevant to the quest for the high goal, but that is not really so; a suitable mode of living and attitude to life are *essential* adjuncts to the main task of spiritual cultivation. What I have not tried to do is to work out in my own mind how a modern man bound by virtually unbreakable ties to life in a great city can hope to adapt the life-style of the Taoist recluses to his needs. It should not prove impossible, but is difficult; I suppose each individual needs to work it out for himself, depending on his actual situation. At the same time, I feel strongly that whoever desires to pursue the Path by Taoist methods should do everything in his power to discover a means of living in some pleasantly remote rural area. A good way to support oneself is to take up some such occupation as carpentry, which has the double advantage of entailing skillful work with a natural material and of making but slight demand on the mental vigor one wishes to conserve for yogic contemplation.

Mode of living Since nothing lies outside the Tao, the painful sounds of traffic and road-menders' drills, the stink of petrol and similar obstacles to quiet peacefulness are as much the Tao as the tinkle of mountain streams or the smell of jasmine; therefore neither urban surroundings nor the lack of a few like-minded friends should prevent one from cultivating the Way successfully; but I think one would need to be an advanced adept to be able to ignore such circumstances. In China, Taoist recluses live in small communities in rural surroundings remote from the busy market-place, but not so remote as to create great difficulty in supplying their simple wants. For esoteric reasons connected with *fêng shui* (wind and water science or geomancy), the hermitage sites are chosen to accord with "nature's influences," usually with rising ground behind and running water to the front, i.e. the south. Hilly or mountainous places remarkable for natural beauty are preferred, especially if there is a waterfall or cascade in the neighborhood, some picturesque rock-formations, and pines or clumps of feathery bamboo, both of which have poetical associations for the Chinese. The buildings combine beauty with absence of ostentation and fit the surroundings as if they too were part of nature; within their courtyards or the outer gardens will invariably be found miniature landscapes fashioned from cunningly arranged rocks and pools.

Whatever the surroundings, an absolute requirement is that simplicity and moderation (but certainly not drabness) form the keynotes of the adepts' way of living – frugal but tasty food; perhaps a little wine, but never drunkenness; serviceable and even picturesque garments and furniture, but never ostentation or frivolous expense. There may be objects of beauty – a charming tea-set or set of writing implements, a porcelain vase or two for holding blooms or blossom-bearing branches, calligraphic scrolls or landscape paintings on the walls, and windows cut in the shape of a full moon, a maple leaf, a vase, a bell and so on, provided these few luxuries are acquired without extravagance and not so dwelt upon that their loss would occasion much regret. Better austerity than profusion; to care much about possessions or greatly desire what is not there is known to be harmful to cultivation of the Way. Relative poverty is preferred to excess of wealth or a clutter of possessions, but unnecessarily harsh privation or deliberately self-imposed hardship is avoided like any other kind of extreme. Excess in either direction cannot go together with moderation.

In such communities, the rules imposed are minimal. Since chores and cooking must be seen to, set meal times and fixed stints of work are found necessary; but the general principle is that the more rules there are, the more the possibilities of transgression; the aim is *to let everyone be himself and do his own thing* as far as the exigencies of harmonious communal living permit. The Way has to be revered and meditated upon, but also *lived*.

Exercise forms an important part of the curriculum, but should not be of a forced kind. Strain and sudden, ungraceful movements are avoided. *T'ai chi ch'uan* (a kind of dancing-cum-shadow boxing), gardening, mountain walks and special yogic exercises are all popular, but not games that encourage rivalry. The very early morning is considered the best time for exercises concerned with cultivation, for a reason connected with beliefs about the circulation of *ch'i* (cosmic or vital energy). Indoor recreations thought to be conducive to cultivation include calligraphy, painting, music (of kinds appreciated for their melody, not for the sake of noise or powerfully emphasized rhythm), handicrafts and *wei ch'i* (Japanese, *go*). The study and practice of traditional Chinese medicine and poetic or philosophical composition are also favorite pursuits. (There are hermitages where healing, exorcism, spirit evocation, divinations and religious rituals are pursued, mainly as a means of earning support for the community but these are generally eschewed as by-paths of sacred learning by those who seek the high goal of mystical attainment.)

Attitude Few recluses are capable of spending all their waking hours rapt in yogic contemplation; hence, unswerving pursuit of the main goal requires the development of a general attitude to everything that happens which will tend to make all the adept's activities a part of his overall yogic practice. Again, simplicity and moderation form the keynotes. To win the tranquility and equilibrium needed for high yogic endeavor, one must grow away from acquisitiveness, jealousy, envy, inordinate desire, and of course, any tendency towards anger, rage, or harshness in speech or thought. The adept seeks to become indifferent to gain or loss, fame or blame, and all such pairs of opposites; while following a regime to promote health, vigor and long life, he must not be at all dismayed by illness or the approach of death; but this must not be achieved by suppressing feeling and turning into a block of wood or lump of stone; becoming apathetic would lead to the very opposite of success. He should be warmly receptive to natural beauty, but to rain and snow or wind and thunder no less than sunshine; therefore, he spends some time each day observing nature's rhythms and manifestations, seeing them as integral parts of the workings of the Tao. There is even a form of meditation in which the adept seeks to enter into the being of, say, a tree to the point at which he experiences a merging of his own identity with that of the object of contemplation!

When there is work to do, whether creative work or just some humble chore, it must be done for its own sake – that is, as well as possible without any thought of personal success. In every kind of activity, the Taoist principle is that of *wu wei*. Literally "non-action" or "no action," this term is used to mean avoidance of any action that goes beyond responding as effectively and economically as possible to a current need, rather as a tree grows towards the sunniest spot spontaneously, not as a result of carefully planned action. *Wu wei* implies going with the grain, swimming with the current, not against; that is, taking not the easiest way to gain one's object, but the smoothest and most effective way, the most economical in terms of effort. To do this well, a full knowledge of one's capabilities, one's tools, and the material worked upon is needed; shoddy work may be economical, but it is not *wu wei*. The action of flowing water is held up as the perfect example of *wu wei*; for water's way of dealing with an obstacle is to find a way around it, if possible; failing that, it overcomes the obstruction by imperceptibly eroding it, not by the kind of fierce frontal attack made by wind or fire. (All metaphors have but a limited validity; the Taoist notion of the activity of water does not, I think, extend to the pounding of waves upon a crumbling shore; besides, that is an activity involving wind as well as water.)

The Buddhist concept, "right livelihood," does not receive special mention in Taoist classics. Even so, it is obvious that, if one is forced to go on earning a living while cultivating the Tao, some jobs are much more fitting than others. Even to begin to cultivate the Tao while actively engaged in the rat race is out of the question. A salesman attached to a go-getting firm or a slaughterhouse worker who desires in all sincerity to cultivate the Tao will surely have to begin by finding a new job; and I rather think the same would apply to a soldier or politician. Examples of jobs well suited to cultivation are gardening, husbandry, forestry, or guarding a reservoir. Their being somewhat humble tasks is, of course, a very great advantage.

The virtue of compassion is less emphasized by Taoists than by Buddhists, but success in cultivation demands respect for life and for the natural environment;

any mode of living not consonant with these would severely hinder success.

The "Yoga of Internal Alchemy" This is often an extremely important, but perhaps not an essential part of the main practice. It is held to be a powerfully effective way of achieving the minor goals of health, prolonged or restored youthful vigour and longevity; and also a valuable adjunct to attaining the high goal known as Return to the Source. Unfortunately, successful practice of this yoga, which involves breathing and visualization techniques, is absolutely impossible without the assistance of an experienced teacher, and such men are now most difficult to find. This applies equally to the Green Dragon White Tiger Yoga, for which a partner of the opposite sex is required. Both aim at generating within the body a plentiful supply of *ch'i* (vital energy) and drawing it up to a point near the crown of the head in a manner analogous to *kundalini* yoga. They are mentioned here, partly on account of their importance in the curriculum of Taoist recluses, and partly on account of a very valuable lesson that can be derived merely from knowing something about them; namely that conservation of the seminal fluid is essential to success in yogic contemplation. *Ch'i*, though present in the air we breathe, is found in its most concentrated form near the base of the spine and the sexual fluids of male and female are its principle vehicle within the human body. If these fluids are frequently expended, failure to achieve the minor goals, let alone the highest goal, is inevitable. Since moderation is the keynote and total abstention is extreme, it was the practice of Taoist hermits to "return to the world" for a short period each year. In this, as in all other matters, one should not be rigid, but high yogic endeavor to achieve man's ultimate goal in a single lifetime does demand the sacrifice of transient pleasures and particular attention should be given to the conservation of *ch'i*. Happily, as the spiritual faculties develop and become refined, the desire for sensual and emotional satisfaction wanes like the stars when a full moon floods the skies, so no long-lasting hardship is entailed.

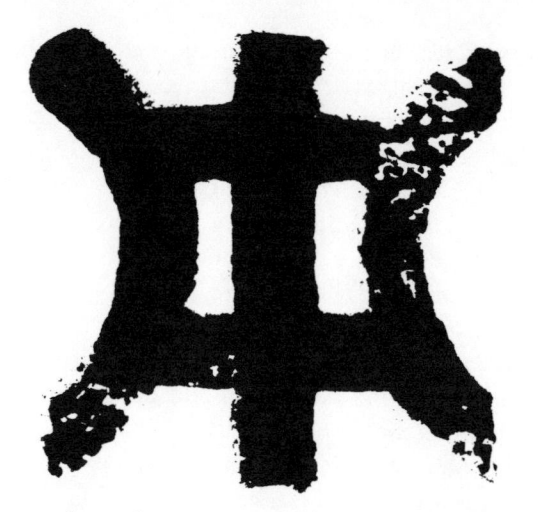

The main practice: contemplative yoga In an important sense, mode of living, attitude, recreation and occupation are themselves part of the main practice, since the necessary tranquility of mind can never be attained for as long as the craving for worldly satisfactions persists; whereas from tranquility proceeds a smiling acceptance of change, of high and low, of good and evil fortune, health and sickness, life and death. Yet, according to the mystics who practice Return to the Source, even perfect tranquility is but a means to the one great end; from first to last, one must engage in contemplative yoga. For this, as for other yogas, an experienced teacher is greatly to be desired; but, unlike those others, it *can* be practiced on one's own, or at least a start can be made in preparation for the time when a teacher is found. Books on meditation are helpful at the beginning; and there are teachers of Chinese Ch'an, of Soto Zen (which does not use koans) and of the various branches of the Tibetan Vajrayana who, without being Taoists, teach methods close enough to the Taoist methods to be similarly effective. Sects and -isms become increasingly of less consequence as the higher stages of mystical experience are attained.

Of the various methods of yogic contemplation (now popularly called meditation as distinct from forms with more active physical components which are popularly called yoga), those employed by Taoists require much fuller and much more detailed instructions than can be derived from what follows. Here, the purpose is to give a preliminary view of a wide field of practice.

There are some Taoists who teach that practices involving breathing techniques and/or inward turned contemplation should be preceded by or alternated with a simple quietistic practice that is probably of great antiquity. Normally, this takes two forms. (1) One sits in a pleasant outdoor spot gazing upon some natural vista and causing the mind to grow still. Presently the perception arises that the Tao is like a mysterious wind or current interfusing the myriad forms, all of which are one with it in substance. The mind sinks into the vista and directly achieves a marvelous intuition of being at one with the objects of its attention. Sky and water, trees and rocks do not fade from consciousness, but the notion of one who contemplates vanishes and the adept, as it were, *becomes* an integral part of the whole scene, a tree- or rock-like extension of the knoll on which he sits. No trace of I and it, or I and they remains. (2) Everything is done and happens as before, except that one particular tree or rock formation is chosen as the object and the adept enters a state of consciousness wherein he, as it were, *becomes* that tree or rock. The latter practice is undertaken over a long period under all sorts of seasonal and weather conditions so that the identity of man and tree can be perfected.

Inward turned contemplation is performed in a clean, quiet place; if it is to be done indoors, it is preferable to set apart a small room, or at least one corner of a room, exclusively for that purpose – a place henceforth unsullied by impure activities or thoughts. There may be, say, a statue of Lao-tzû or the Pole Star deity or some other revered being, or else perhaps a representation of the *yin* and *yang* symbol or of the I Ching trigrams for Heaven and Earth(☰ and ☷), but Taoists cultivating Return to the Source do not regard anything of the kind as essential, unless the *yin* and *yang* symbol is being used in connection with a special course of meditation on the interaction of those two principles. There is usually an incense tripod filled with ash into which one or three sticks of incense are inserted in accordance with ancient tradition. This helps to create a suitable atmosphere, but is far from essential. If incense is used, it should be neither very sweet nor very pungent, but have a rather "austere aroma."

Wrong posture is thought to inhibit the flow of *ch'i* and the postures usually preferred are those which, in the West, now go by the names "full-lotus" and "half-lotus." It is preferable to sit on a large, firm cushion on which a smaller cushion is placed just under the buttocks to reduce pressure on the crossed legs. However, there is no rigidity about the rules for posture. People with injuries to leg or spine and those who take up the practice late in life are advised to meditate while seated upright on a hard chair with the upper part of their legs parallel to the ground. Torturing oneself to sit correctly is not advisable, unless there is a good chance that the position will become comfortable with practice. The trunk must be held erect, but never stiffly. The hands may be held palm upward, resting one upon another with the tips of the thumbs joined to promote circulation of *ch'i;* or they may rest side by side, knuckles upward, fists very lightly clenched, the left thumb extended and loosely grasped by the right first. Belts should be removed, garments loosened; if it is very cold, legs and feet should be protected by the skirts of a long recluse's robe, or by some makeshift such as a small rug. The lips should be gently closed; the teeth lightly touching, not clenched; the tip of the tongue lying effortlessly against the palate.

The upper eyelids should be lowered as a precaution against distraction, but the eyes should not be quite closed for fear of falling asleep.

On taking up one's posture prior to each bout of contemplation, one should mentally envision the sublime goal, visualizing the immaculate Tao in the form of all-pervading light, or as a stream of light flowing through the adept's being (though he must be well aware of the real identity of the flowing Tao and the body through which it flows). At the outset, the contemplation periods need not be more than from twenty to thirty minutes in the morning and again in the early evening; but they should be absolutely regular – that is, never missed or abridged and, as far as possible, always at the same time of day. As progress is made, both the length and number of daily contemplation periods should be extended.

The ultimate objective is so exalted that only a vague preconception of it is possible, but it may be described as direct intuitive experience of such total immersion in the undifferentiated Tao that not one particle of selfness and otherness remains, just an all-pervading unity wherein the entire universe is recognized as a seamless extension of one's being (or, rather, wherein one's being is totally absorbed into the whole). With the vanishing of "self and other," the light of the Tao is perceived as shining unimpededly throughout the universe; there is no longer any sense of its being inside or outside; it just *is!* One should bear this objective in mind from the very start, although many preliminary stages must first be attained.

The stages are not fixed in kind or number, but depend upon the wisdom and experience of one's teacher. Often they begin with simple exercises for achieving one-pointedness of mind similar to those used by Buddhists and other mystics, such as counting the breath while breathing slowly and softly. Sometimes the earlier steps are of a more "scientific" kind. Having made a study of books dealing with the interaction of *yin* and *yang*, one alternately contemplates certain natural phenomena and meditates upon their production by *yin-yang* interaction, or uses some quite different method aimed at understanding the essential unity of opposites. Sometimes the whole course of contemplation from beginning to end is based on the need to transcend all notions of duality in order to attain the ultimate goal, this being one of many Taoist techniques which influenced the development of Ch'an (Zen).

The breathing techniques which usually follow the most elementary stage of training are characteristically Taoist, differing in important aspects from those used in Buddhist yogas, although stimulation of the flow of *ch'i* by visualizing it as flowing through certain psychic channels is analogous in a general way to Buddhist techniques and achieves identical results. Many kinds of Taoist contemplation involve giving one's whole attention to certain specific places within the adept's body, such as the Mysterious Pass of the Precious Square Inch which lies just behind the mid-point between the eyes. This may lead to a sensation of brilliant light emanating from the point contemplated and flooding through the body. Though this is an auspicious sign of progress, it can become an obstacle if it is permitted to distract the adept's attention. At all times, the mind must remain free from the duality of consciousness and object of consciousness, so that it may return to the primeval state of awareness which Lao-tzû termed the Uncarved Block. Even in cases where the meditator is not instructed to concentrate on the Mysterious Pass, success in contemplation often results in sensations of pure light shining within, the appearance of inner lightning flashes, and the sound of inner thunder. The occurence of such phenomena is encouraging, but they should not be dwelt upon unduly and most certainly not mistaken for the dawn of the ultimate experience!

Some teachers hold that the results of contemplation of the Mysterious Pass are dangerously distracting and so prefer other methods. One of these is known as Alternating Contemplation of the Mother and Child, a reference to Lao-tzû's great work, wherein "the Mother" is the name given to the pure, undifferentiated Tao, whereas "the Child" is the Tao as the totality of form. Turn by turn, one seeks to perceive the void by cultivating objectless awareness and to penetrate to the very essence of form by contemplating natural phenomena, the rhythm of the seasons, the flux of change governing one's own life and so on. At a later stage, one penetrates beyond duality; void is perceived as form, form as void. The stage is thus set for the ultimate experience.

Whatever techniques are chosen, knowledge, logic, discrimination, analysis, and reason must be perceived from the first as obstacles to intuition and banished during contemplation. Later, self-consciousness is anihilated and replaced by vivid, immediate, intuitive awareness of the unity of thinking, thought and thinker, of beholding, beheld and beholder. Free from dualistic thought and ego-delusion, the mind undergoes a liberating transformation, whereupon the ego is recognized as a poor ghost of what never was or ever will be. Limpid perception now dawns and the Tao is manifested as penetrating, encompassing, interfusing the myriad forms and simultaneously as being the very "stuff" of which they are composed. The "close-to-ultimate" experience may take the form of being lost in the purity of voidness, wherein darting tongues of flaming color shoot forth like dancing or contending dragons, presently comingling and giving birth, perhaps, to a universe of spinning globules whirling to an ecstatic rhythm – throughout all of which there is no sense of view and viewer, for the viewer *is* what he views. Or else, the adept's mind functions like a universal mirror impartially reflecting the changing scene. Things pass endlessly across its surface, leaving no trace of their passing. Sensations of all-pervading light, of elation, of bodily lightness may supervene, culminating in a period of ecstasy. On returning towards a more "everyday" state of consciousness, one recalls having perceived the Tao and dwelt in its inner stillness – timeless, formless, all-pervading. One has by now actually experienced with crystal clarity that, apart from that limitless totality, things have no being. The Tao and the myriad forms *are not two*. No longer a mere concept learnt from one's teachers, this has become a direct perception resulting from perfect non-awareness of a self that looks. More than that even, it will now be apparent that the Tao, besides being the totality of forms, besides being perceiver and perceived, is also *wholly contained in each and every form! Your own mind, therefore, is the universe itself!*

One who has experienced Return to the Source does not, at death, slip like a dew-drop "into the shining sea." He *is* the entirety of that limitless ocean! With the casting off of the physical body, no shadow of illusion remains. Adept and universe are one!

KAREL WERNER

Spiritual Personality and its Formation according to Indian Tradition

INDIAN tradition has developed a unique conception of what we have vaguely circumscribed in the title as "spiritual personality." Its uniqueness lies in the claim that a man who has developed it has reached, here and now, a state of perfection, maturity and inner understanding of reality which is definite, complete, and universal. Other traditions have their saints and mystics striving for unity with God, but India, besides having mystics, has also produced perfect spiritual personalities who appear to have climbed the ladder of spiritual development as free individuals. Having seen that worldly pursuits lead only to temporary satisfactions, they decide to work for the high and permanent spiritual achievement of perfection using methods of systematic spiritual training based on a universally valid law.

This achievement of the Indian tradition has not been brought about gradually in the process of evolution of Indian spirituality; rather we find it in India in the oldest times and witness it as a recurring phenomenon throughout the centuries of India's history till the present day. The actual method, discipline, or path which takes the individual to the goal has undergone numerous modifications and reformulations, but the core is always the same. We shall now try to trace the more important formulations of the discipline and goal in subsequent historical epochs.

The earliest spiritual giants of the Indian tradition, some four thousand years ago, were the ancient seers (*ṛṣis*) whose penetrating vision (*dhīti*) of reality in its totality was far above the grasp of the minds of average men of the time. So they expressed their vision in verses full of symbolical meaning and mythological imagery which could make a direct impact on the minds and hearts of people and thus guide their lives. That is how the Vedas originated, and their influence was so strong that they came to be regarded as holy scriptures and have been preserved as such till the present day in a form virtually unchanged since their codification around 1000 B.C.

It is only natural that the wisdom of the Vedic seers was not fully grasped and that their successors, unable to realize the full meaning of the hymns, used them more for liturgical purposes as prayers and sacrificial texts rather than for stimulating their inner spiritual growth. There is, however, clear evidence that even during the centuries following the early age of enlightened seers while generations of priests (*brāhmans*) indulged in excessive ritualism the achievement of personal spiritual maturity was not lost to all but was maintained by sages (*munis*) who lived apart from the established society as homeless wanderers. Owing to their appearance they were called "the long-haired ones" (*keśins*) and were evidently in great esteem among the people, although not popular with priests. One late Vedic hymn (RV 10, 136), composed obviously by a liberal-minded *brāhman*, describes the phenomenon of *keśins* and reveals a lot about their ways and achievements. The hymn goes as follows:

1. The long-haired one carries within himself fire and poison and both heaven and earth. To look at him is like seeing heavenly brightness in its fullness. He is said to be light itself.

2. The sages, girdled with the wind, are clad in dust of

yellow hue. They follow the path of the wind when the gods have penetrated them.

3. "Uplifted by our sagehood we have ascended upon the winds. You mortals see just our bodies."

4. The sage flies through the inner region, illuminating all forms below. Dedicated to holy work he is a friend of every god.

5. Being the wind's horse, the friend of *Vāyu* and god-inspired, the sage is at home in both oceans, the eastern and the western.

6. Wandering in the track of celestial beings and sylvan beasts, the long-haired one, knowing their aspiration, is a sweet and most uplifting friend.

7. For him *Vāyu* churned, even pounded that which is hard to bend, as the long-haired one drank poison with the cup, togther with Rudra.

This is obviously a portrait of a true spiritual being who has mastered the opposite poles of spiritual creativity and bliss (symbolized by fire and heaven) on the one hand and of the painful agony of earthly existence (expressed by the image of poison and earth) on the other and has become an embodiment of the inner light of wisdom for others to see. He lives outside society and its conventions and goes about naked, clad only in the yellow dust of the Indian soil and "girdled" with the wind. He is called *muni* (sage), because he frequently spends his time in musing or meditating (*man*), and his path is not of this world. Like the mysterious wind he can not be traced, and he is carried by cosmic forces (*devas*) which penetrate him when his mind experiences freedom from earth-bound involvements. He asserts in a direct statement that he and others like him have developed, through spiritual practice (*mauneya*), a status which is beyond the comprehension of ordinary people. The words, "You mortals see just our bodies" indicate that their status is one of immortality. In other words, they have shifted the center of experience of themselves from the sheath of the material body with which ordinary people identify themselves (being therefore mortals) into the sheath of a spiritual body which is not subjected to dying. With this body they move in the inner region (*antarikṣan*), a dimension of reality which is superior to the material sphere and in which the sage sees and understands "all forms" or archetypes of everything that exists, sharing his knowledge with gods. More psychologically expressed: the sage reaches, through spiritual endeavor (*saukṛtya*), the power to illuminate the contents of the unconscious mind from the superior position of an enlightened one. The individual unconscious mind overlaps with the cosmic mind (inner region) with its archetypal forms and is the matrix of visible reality (later known in the Yogācāra school of Mahāyāna Buddhism as *ālaya vijñāna* – store consciousness). Therefore, self-knowledge gained through meditation amounts to universal knowledge of reality from within.

The sage is thus one with life at large, both as far as biological vitality is concerned (being the horse or vehicle of the wind: *Vāta= prāṇa*, i.e., life force in its lower aspect) and also with respect to the cosmic force of life itself (as the friend of *Vāyu= prāṇa* in its higher aspect), and he is penetrated or inspired by divine forces. Consequently he is at home both in the realm of light (eastern ocean) and in the realm of darkness (western ocean), i.e., he has mastered the forces of life both on the spiritual and on the material level (as later Mahāyāna Bodhisattvas who have attained *nirvāṇa* and at the same time continue being active in *saṁsāra*). As an enlightened one the sage is naturally able to follow the tracks of all beings, superhuman as well as subhuman. He knows their hearts, and understanding them, he is their best friend, who can help and uplift them. The image of a sweet friend is again reminiscent of the later Buddhist concept of a "beautiful" or spiritual friend (*kalyāna mitra*), an expression used for the personal teacher in some Mahāyāna Buddhist circles.

The last verse of the hymn expresses once again, in mythological allusions, the basic principles and events of the spiritual achievement of the highest order which the *muni* accomplished and what this means for the world at large. The image of churning refers to the purāṇic myth according to which the gods, originally mortal, churned the world ocean in order to obtain the drink of immortality. This symbolizes the struggle of mortal beings for an achievement which has been their aspiration ever since they realized their mortal status and which is expressed, in one form or another, in mythologies and religious allegories of all times and all nations. The *keśin*, having reached harmony with universal life (as *Vāyu's* friend), achieved immortality in a way which, with hindsight, appears to have been spontaneous (*Vāyu* did it for him). The purāṇic myth further reveals that, during the churning of the world ocean before the drink of immortality was won, poison was released as a by-product of the churning. Poison symbolizes the unavoidable phenomenon of death within the universe (as Buddhism later asserts: *saṁsāra* is the realm of *Māra*), but the *keśin* overcame death by shifting his consciousness from the material to the spiritual level of existence. He reached immortality while still active in (drinking from) the stream of mortal (poisonous) life in the material world. (To repeat it again in Buddhist parlance: having realized *nirvāṇa*, he remained active in *saṁsāra*, untouched by its defilements.)

In the purāṇic story the gods were horrified by the poison, and it was only Śiva (a later name of Rudra) who drank the poison without harm and thus became the savior of beings. But Śiva, known among other things as *Yogapati*, the Lord of Yoga, symbolizes in Hindu mythology spiritual progress through individual yogic effort and the power to assist other beings by helping them to overcome the deadly stream of samsāric existence. The image of drinking the poison in Rudra's company therefore suggests again the idea of assistance which the *keśin* gives to others. Here we have the earliest expression of the double role of the spiritual path: to save oneself, and to help others reach salvation through a kind of self-sacrifice by descending into lower levels of existence from the height of absolute redemption. In Hinduism it has found an expression in the doctrine of divine incarnations (*avatāras*), while Buddhism spelled it out in the form of the teaching of the sequence of Buddhas (Hīnayāna school) and in the form of the Bodhisattva doctrine (Mahāyāna school).

This short ancient hymn comprises the whole essence of the Indian spiritual tradition, and all subsequent doctrines are elaborations of what is fundamentally implicit in it. What it does not contain is the method, the instructions for practice which were presumably obtained orally when an aspirant joined an accomplished master on his wanderings or in his forest hermitage. And as we can gather from the Āraṇyakas, Upaniṣads and Pāli Buddhist scriptures, there were many teachers and schools of spiritual practice or Yoga in ancient times, and they all had their distinct methods of training. The Upaniṣads mention some of the elements and stages of the practice, and so does the Buddha (563–483 B.C.), who had stayed in various schools of Yoga prior to his enlightenment. When he afterwards become a teacher himself, he concentrated on expounding to his pupils just the path towards *nirvāṇa* or spiritual realization, leaving unanswered all questions concerning the ultimate nature of that realization and other philosophical questions. Because he attracted a vast following and because a whole new religion, now known as Buddhism, developed in his wake, a large number of his discourses has been preserved and in them, both general and detailed instructions for spiritual practice. The backbone of this practice is the so-called Noble Eightfold Path (*ariya aṭṭhaṅgika magga*) which is the oldest known comprehensive formulation of a Yoga path, i.e. a method of transforming and spiritualizing human personality.

The Buddha's eightfold path is a masterpiece of psychological insight and methodical ingenuity. It proceeds to form and develop man's personality using three main avenues: that of knowledge and wisdom (*paññā*), that of morality or ethical behavior (*sīla*), and that of meditation or absorption (*samādhi*). The first one is described by two parts of the path: right viewing (*sammā diṭṭhi*) and right thinking (*sammā saṅkappa*). The prevailing view of experienced reality which every living being takes is utilitarian: of what use is this or that to me? Does it serve my survival, satisfy my needs, enhance my prospects for success in the world? The Buddha, in fact, did not discard this basic attitude, but taught his pupils to view things from the standpoint of *absolute* utility: the final goal of freedom. That requires transcending narrow temporary aims and viewing the things of life in the context of the whole of reality. With this attitude all thinking and all resolutions gradually change, and the whole life of the individual turns in the direction of the final goal, enabling man to fulfill the second aspect of the training which concerns ethical behavior and is described as right speech (*sammā vāca*), right acting (*sammā kammanta*) and right livelihood (*sammā ājīva*).

All these steps when consistently applied have a profound influence on the formation of a new inner personality. But the inner training proper is represented by mental endeavor. Its first prerequisite is right effort (*sammā vāyāma*), whose importance cannot be overestimated. It expresses the necessity for the employment of volitional exertion on the spiritual path and also the fact that the process of spiritual maturing is, not automatic or spontaneous (at least to begin with) but a matter of choosing it and working for it with determination until the vision of the goal is so strong that deviation from the path is impossible. The method of spiritual training carried by right effort is defined by right mindfulness (*sammā sati*). It is a state of watchful awareness of what is going on in the trainee's mind so that he knows of his thoughts, feelings, and reactions when they occur and is not governed by them, but himself determines their course. In the process of developing this self-awareness, he gets to know more and more of his previously hidden motivations and tendencies of his unconscious mind until the whole of his mind becomes illuminated by the light of full consciousness, and he reaches perfect self-knowledge. This process of self-illumination has a deep influence on the personality which becomes transformed and purified. It is paralleled, through the application of the eighth part of the path, right absorption (*sammā samādhi*), by the deepening and widening of mental experience on a level which is no longer purely individual but includes the dimensions of the cosmic. Proceeding through four stages of concrete absorptions (*rūpa jhānas*), one reaches a state of perfect equilibrium (*upekkhā*) which is a basis for the development of extraordinary powers (*siddhis*), four further states of mind known as abstract absorptions (*arūpa jhānas*) which are cosmic-orientated and, finally, for taking the last step towards liberation, the achievement of *nirvāṇa*.

A few centuries after the Buddha, Patañjali summarized the teachings of Yoga schools of old and of his time in a slender volume known as *Yoga Sūtra* which is still *the* classical exposition of the spiritual path to liberation. It is more compact and technical than the Buddha's path, but both systems show close similarities which point to a common background. Patañjali's system is also eightfold (*aṣṭaṅga yoga*) and starts with two steps which concern the development of the moral foundations of personality. They are *yama*, consisting of five abstentions (from killing, lying, stealing, sexual misconduct and appropriating), and *niyama*, comprising five observances (of purity, contentment, exertion, self-development and surrender to the divine). In the third and fourth step our attention is turned towards our physical organism. *Āsana* or posture requires from the Yogi the ability of assuming a steady meditational position which, in India, has always been crosslegged. *Prāṇāyāma* is a discipline of breath control. Since there is an obvious close connection between the flow of breathing and the working of the mind, the importance of controlled breathing in connection with mind development is obvious.

The subsequent four steps of Patañjali's Yoga represent a gradual process of awakening the mind for the inner perception of truth. It is a sequence of mental exercises which shows the masterliness of Patañjali's knowledge of the Yoga technique. What is required first is *pratyāhāra* or withdrawal of attention from the senses and the endless flow of thoughts, ideas and imaginings usually filling the mind. This is followed by applying *dhāraṇā* or concentration focused on one particular object of the mind's internal experience whereby "one pointedness" (*ekāgratā*) of the mind is developed, which is in deep contrast to the usual distracted state of mind. With a one pointed mind firmly established, the next step, called *dhyāna* (contemplation) is reached. It is a state of deep awareness in which any image, idea or experience on which the mind focuses is seen "from inside"; *dhyāna* is direct cognition of the essence of the contemplated object. The final step is known as *samādhi*, or full unification of the Yogi's being with his cognition. Here, to be is to know and to know is to be, with respect so oneself (which equals total self-knowledge) as well as to reality as a whole (which equals total enlightenment, the discovery of the essential oneness of the individual and the universal). As in Buddhist Yoga, the *samādhi* of Patañjali's system is a complex experience with stages of ever increasing depth resulting eventually in the complete autonomy (*kaivalya*) of the personality which equals its final liberation (*mokṣa*) from the categories of limited existence.

In the period following Patañjali's achievement, Yoga as a personal quest for truth and salvation became very popular and came to be incorporated into the wider system of Hindu religious practices as their higher aspect, thus coming nearer to what we know from other religious traditions as mysticism, which defines its aim as union or coming face to face with God. The best source for popularized Yoga is the *Bhagavad Gītā* which treats various aspects of Yoga almost as separate types of Yoga, and their respective methodological features were then further developed. Four of them are of major importance:

1. *Karma Yoga* is based on the idea that action in one form or another is unavoidable and that it is even unsuitable for most people to try to renounce their duties in the world as most Yogis did in ancient India. What is important when one acts, however, is the motivation of action and its wisdom or foolishness. Driven by selfish desire (*kāma*) or anger (*krodha*) man acts foolishly and becomes entangled deeper and deeper in the karmic net. The path of Karma Yoga is the path of unselfish action involving the renunciation of personal aims when acting. All acting is done without attachment and according to what is correct under the circumstances and within the framework of the universal welfare. Such action does not bind (as creating the world does not bind God), and eventually a state of complete freedom is reached.

2. *Dyhāna Yoga* is the path of meditation, and it requires regular meditational sittings even when one leads a busy life. During the sittings one calms one's breathing, checks the thinking process within the mind, and focuses it on the Divine (*Brahman*) within oneself. *Dhyāna* or meditative perception is gradually extended from the periods of quiet sitting into the active periods and eventually becomes a way of life.

3. *Jñāna Yoga* proceeds by way of discriminative knowledge which means sorting out what is essential,

and therefore eternal and real, from what is non-essential, i.e., temporary and, in the last instance, unreal. The final knowledge then presents itself to the Yogi in the form of a direct realization of the essential unity of existence in which, however, the eternal existence of the (transformed) person (*puruṣa*) of the Yogi is maintained. This is a mystery to be solved only by inward experience. It completely defies attempts to present it in conceptual terms. Hence the three different expositions of this philosophy known as Vedāntism by three different philosophers: the non-dualism (*Advaita*) of Śankara, the qualified non-dualism (*Viśiṣṭādvaita*) of Rāmanuja and the dualism (*Dvaita*) of Madhva.

For the practical application of Jñāna Yoga the conceptual understanding of the mystery of the final experience is irrelevant. The Bhagavad Gītā simply recommends that everything should be seen as stemming from the Divine, which is to be regarded as the changeless essence behind changing forms. The best systematic elaboration of the Jñāna Yoga technique is that of Śankara. It has four basic requirements: (i) Discrimination (*viveka*) is the one already referred to. (ii) Dispassionateness (*vairāgya*) requires that the Yogi guard himself against becoming possessed, infatuated, and eventually even slightly disturbed by passions and moods of the mind related to sensual desire and attachments. (iii) Six attainments (*ṣatsampati*) have to be acquired in the process of intense self-education in tranquillity (*sama*), self-control in acting (*dama*), eradication of the eagerness to possess (*uparati*), patience (*titikṣā*), confidence or sincerity (*śraddhā*) and intentness of the mind (*samādhāna*). (iv) Finally there must be a deep longing (not to say passion) for liberation (*mumukṣatva*) which indicates that a mere superficial or half-hearted interest will not lead far on the path.

The training in the four requirements may be gradual and it proceeds through three stages. The first is hearing (*śravaṇa*) or studying the teaching "at the feet of a master" or by reading; the second is thinking or "mentation" (*manena*), i.e. letting the teaching "sink in" through intellectually analyzing it and then applying it to oneself; and finally comes the stage of "constant meditation" (*nididhyāsana*) when the teaching has been absorbed and a new outlook on reality developed, allowing the Yogi to experience its inner dimension directly.

4. *Bhakti Yoga* is the path of Divine love and love for the Divine and centers around the belief in, and a fully admitted dependence on, a personal God as the highest aim of man's spiritual pilgrimage. God stands here for the ultimate reality expounded in other systems in an impersonal form as *Brahman, Ātman, Nirvāṇa, Śūnyatā* etc. Some people cannot be inspired to spiritual endeavor by philosophical concepts of the transcendent and systematic instructions for spiritual training but are able to summon considerable resources for the work of transforming their personalities if they can relate themselves to the ultimate in the form of a most perfect person, i.e. God, through the bond of love. In this respect Bhakti Yoga is the nearest equivalent to Christian mysticism and Islamic sufism. But the Bhagavad Gītā which is the chief advocate of it insists that there is no essential difference between a personal God and the impersonal transcendent goal of other Yoga systems. We are faced here with the mystery of the nature of the ultimate which, philosophically understood, is beyond all concepts of personality and yet at the same time possesses all that is usually associated with the notion of a supreme personality called God or the Lord.

The personal bond of love in Bhakti Yoga is made possible by the presentation of the ultimate or God in the form of a divine incarnation (*avatāra*) on earth. In the Bhagavad Gītā it is *Kṛṣṇa* who expounds the teaching and is represented as the supreme Lord, at the same time human and loving as well as transcendent and identical with the infinite and eternal nature of ultimate reality. The path to him as Lord leads through a life of devotional surrender. Every thought, emotion, word, and deed becomes an act of sacrifice directed towards the Lord. The total giving up of one's personality is to bring about eventually an awareness of universality and liberation from the limited form of existence, just as on the methodical paths of other schools.

In the process of further elaboration of various aspects of Yoga practice, some special types of Yoga emerged, such as *Hatha Yoga* which concentrates on physical and breathing exercises and *Kuṇḍalinī Yoga* which tries to utilize, for the purpose of spiritual progress to perfection, the energy of the subtle body known as *kuṇḍalinī*. This is guided along a channel (*suṣumna*) parallel to the spine through spiritual centers (*cakras*) until it reaches the center of enlightenment at the top of the skull known as the "thousand-petalled lotus" (*sahasrara padma*) and brings about the corresponding experience. Since this spiritual energy (*kuṇḍalinī śakti*) is believed to be essentially the same creative energy that, on the cosmic level, brings about the manifestation of the universe and that is, in unawakened man, responsible for his sexual and procreational potency, a view was developed that man's sexual energy could be directly utilized for the purpose of his spiritual progress. Thus *Tantric Yoga* emerged, a mysterious and as yet very little explored territory of Indian religious and Yogic tradition. It appears that it is split into two schools of thought and practice. If the sexual energy is utilized by being transformed into pure spiritual energy, one speaks about right-hand Tantric Yoga. If sexual practices on the physical level are included in the methodical technique of the path with the alleged aim of thereby inducing a direct link to the cosmic creative forces, we are faced with so-called left-hand Tantric practice.

As the centuries passed the struggle and ambition of the human mind to grasp intellectually and realize factually its spiritual potential was continuing in India with undiminished vigor and imagination and with a tendency towards universalism. In setting himself the task of final liberation the truth-seeker was now no longer satisfied with solving it only for himself but expressed his aspiration to include in his final achievement his fellow beings and even the whole universe. The spiritualization of reality in its entirety became the goal. Two instances representative of this trend are (i) the doctrine of Mahāyāna Buddhism and (ii) the teachings of Śrī Aurobindo Ghosh.

The Mahāyāna teachings emerged when the original message of the Buddha came to be understood too narrowly and lost its appeal to the masses. In the new formulation it was no longer the quest for individual perfection (arhatship), following the path of the Buddha as the incomparable teacher, that presented the challenge and stimulus, but the desire or aspiration to help all creatures to reach the same perfection and enlightenment that amounted to Buddahood. The new path became known as that of a Bodhisattva. Once one had come to recognize the urgency of working for spiritual realization on a universal scale, one would make a vow not to enter the state of final liberation (*nirvāṇa*), which would mean leaving the world of suffering (*sasṁāra*) totally behind, until one had helped all other beings, even down to the last blade of grass, to reach that freedom. The scheme of training of a Bodhisattva proceeds in ten stages (*bhūmis*) and requires him to develop qualities known as perfections (*pāramitās*) which make him into a fully and veritably enlightened being.

Setting oneself the task of working for the salvation of others, rather than, as it were, turning one's back on the world and getting on with one's own salvation, may be regarded, in the context of Buddhist development after the Buddha's death, as a kind of safeguard against the self-deception and self-isolation which can easily arise during the struggle of an individual to transcend the world's and other beings' imperfections in the absence of an enlightened teacher. Rigidity of mind may have set in and made monks into pious followers and preservers of the letter of the Buddha's teaching instead of realizing its spirit. The primary aim of a Bodhisattva, however, was to assist others and renounce everything that would bring advantage only to him. Therefore, he did not want anything for himself, not even *nirvāṇa*, although he worked on himself and his own perfection with such earnestness and effort that they were bound to bring him to the very threshold of *nirvāṇa* sooner or later with only a little step left to achieve it. Yet the Bodhisattva would not take that last step and would turn away from *nirvāṇa* in order to stay in *saṁsāra* for the sake of helping others. Paradoxically enough, this very act of renouncing *nirvāṇa* for the sake of others secures it for him in a far superior way than any personal effort to reach his own salvation could do. For such renunciation is certainly the highest possible expression of perfect selflessness. And perfect dissociation from the self and self-centeredness is what *nirvāṇa* is about. As a result of this supreme act of renunciation the Bodhisattva actually finds himself in *nirvāṇa* while at the same time staying and remaining active in *saṁsāra*.

The Bodhisattva doctrine is apparently an expression of the knowledge and intuition regarding the final state of the transformation of the human personality, i.e., that it is not a state of individual isolation but an achievement of universal character. Thus the transformed individual personality finds itself fully linked to universal reality, which is not a distant realm of everlasting perfection unconnected with this world, but this very world which has been transfigured to make it a spiritual abode of perfect beings.

The knowledge or intuition of this possibility, if not inevitability, of the spiritualization of this world brought about through the effort of striving individuals is also the central theme of Aurobindo's philosophical outlook. To Aurobindo individual salvation is a small achievement, especially if it is enjoyed in seclusion or isolation from the rest of a creation left behind by the liberated one. The true salvation to be aimed at includes the salvation or spiritualization of the whole cosmos. Therefore a man who strives after liberation should be preparing himself to become a tool of universal salvation. His preparation takes the form of the spiritual integration of all the constituents of his being with the Divine Supermind. That means that the whole of his personality has to be spiritualized: his mentality, including his intellectual capacity, his life force or vitality – with all its biological instincts – and also his material body. Nothing is abandoned or thrown away in the final integration. The process of spiritual growth is not one of elimination but one of transformation.

An integrated individual who has reached salvation has achieved it not only by getting to know himself in the deeper layers of his mind, that is by reaching perfect self-knowledge which is always an important part of every spiritual training, but also – and more importantly – by opening his mind to the Divine Supermind which lifts him to the status of a Superman or Gnostic Being. This status is above any sense of individuality in terms of self-centeredness or self-interest. The consciousness of a Superman is infinite, his mental faculties are unlimited, and he has a great power for illuminating others and spiritualizing his environment. Yet he does not altogether cease to be an individual, for he will still use a body and will be appearing in the world. His body will not, however, be an autonomous product of nature but, as an integrated part of his personality as a Gnostic Being, will function under the full control of the Supermind with which the Superman is one. On the level of the Divine there is no contradiction between the individual and the universal or between the personal and the impersonal. Both are inseparable aspects of one and the same reality.

Having accomplished the integration and spiritualization of his own personality, Aurobindo's Superman directs his attention to assisting other people towards the same – or perhaps it is better to say towards a similar achievement, for although there is oneness within the Divine, there is no actual sameness among individual Supermen. At the same time the Superman exercizes a spiritualizing influence on all his surroundings: on nature and society, and on their various processes. In the long run, with some Supermen active in the world, the whole world will be spiritualized. A further stage will include the spiritualization of the entire cosmos.

Although this outline of Aurobindo's vision might indicate that the final transformation of the cosmos is bound to come in any case – as a result of a long-term evolution under the influence of the Supermind, it is not so. The Divine mind will not act unless there is a receptacle prepared for it. And the preparation of the receptacles rests with the efforts of individuals. Unless there is at least one integrated individual who has developed his mind and purified his personality to the point of having transcended his individuality, the Supermind will not start working. Thence, only if others follow suit and also achieve the status of Supermen, so that an élite of spiritual beings will appear in the world, can the process of spiritualization of the earth and subsequently of the whole cosmos be set going under the influence of the Supermind.

The Supermind is prepared to descend and work through developed individuals whenever one or more of them reaches the necessary status (although this process must not be viewed as an automatic one). However, if a culture is at a certain stage of evolution which requires a Divine intervention for its preservation and further growth and if the Divine power on descent does not find prepared receptacles, that is, if there are no individuals who have worked sufficiently for their salvation, then the Supermind cannot descend and revitalize that culture, and this will then have tragic consequences.

Śrī Aurobindo's philosophy thus not only presents an individual searching for freedom with the prospect of a high achievement in becoming a Superman but confronts him, at the same time, with a high responsibility for triggering off, or at least contributing to, the final liberation of the whole cosmos.

When we have thus gone, in a brief survey, through some of the best teachings on the formation of spiritual personality produced by Indian tradition, one question inevitably asserts itself to us: what is the relevance of the Indian achievement to modern man, particularly in the context of Western civilization which has by now spread more or less all over the world?

The answer is unequivocal. The Western mind can draw a lesson from the Indian tradition which may help it overcome its present difficulties. The Western mind has developed its intellectual power of grasping and understanding external reality to such a high degree that it is impossible to imagine that it can go any further. It has discovered how external reality works and how it can be manipulated, in other words, it has created science and technology. Science has formulated what is known as "laws of nature," and technology uses that knowledge to make nature serve man's needs. The result has been a rich material civilization and the prospect of more and expanded knowledge of the external universe and more material wealth which might be sufficent for the whole of mankind provided that the specifically human problems of life and existence are equally well understood and mastered. However, the latter condition has not been fulfilled so far, and there does not seem to be a hope that man will understand himself and his problems better if he continues in the same direction as hitherto. Science may bring him still more knowledge about the world, and technology may create even more material riches, together with ever more powerful means of destruction, but this will not contribute to, let alone bring about, the birth of a truly mature and developed man who understands himself and is in harmony with other men and the world at large.

So knowledge of external nature, which is what science is about, is not enough, although it is extremely valuable when wisely applied. But to achieve mastery of his existential situation, man must add to his scientific achievements the knowledge of internal nature, i.e., of his own inner being and of the inner dimension of reality. That is where the Indian tradition comes into the picture. In the variety of its approaches to the problem of inner perception and its cultivation, the Indian tradition has also developed the methods which can lead the mind in that direction without forcing it to compromise its scientific training and the knowledge gained by it. Certain techniques of Yoga, free from any religious commitment or preconceived philosophical views, promise to open new vistas to the mind while allowing it to sustain its scientific attitude and critical approach based on intellectual analysis. It is often wrongly believed that the spiritual growth of the personality requires a rejection of critical intellect, and it is true that some Indian schools of religious practice which may also be using some elements of Yoga technique stress simplicity of mind and complete surrender of their followers to the Divine or to the guru. But the real growth of spirituality and the eventual spiritual maturity of the human personality is not achieved without, let alone against, the critical reasoning capacity of the human intellect, although it is necessary to go beyond it. The task of a Westerner under training is not to reject or throw away his intellect and discard the achievements of his tradition, but to develop his intellect and fully realize its potential in order to be able to transcend it realistically. This is particularly important in the context of modern Western civilization, which is now practically the world civilization. A failure to develop fully one's intellectual potential leaves one immature and unable to make real use of Eastern methods of mind development. On the other hand, if the personality is not developed spiritually and does not acquire some capacity of supra-intellectual vision, it experiences, in the end, a sense of frustration and loss of purpose.

What, then, are the main points in the lesson the Western mind can draw from Indian tradition?

First, we ought to acknowledge that India has presented us with the example of an age-old civilization which has been permeated by, and during some periods of its history even obsessed with, the quest for the Absolute. This quest has not only expressed itself in the form of conventional religions, mystical endeavors, and philosophical inquiry, all of which can also be found in other traditions, but – in India – it has also developed a nearly scientific approach to the Absolute as the supra-sensory and supra-intellectual reality which is beyond description because it is transcendental. It can, nevertheless, be apprehended by man's direct inner experience because it is also immanent – immanent to the human psyche in its deeper layers and to everything that is.

Second, the apprehension of the Absolute can be achieved if a systematic and methodical training known as Yoga is undertaken to develop man's capacity of inner perception. It eventually provides the mind with a clear and reliable, albeit individual, experience of the Absolute which otherwise must remain a mere object of faith (as God does in religion) or of speculation (in various philosophical systems which use different terms for it). Of course, religions and philosophies in India also strive to some extent for a practical apprehension of the Absolute in the form in which they conceive it. Therefore, some kind of Yoga training has been incorporated in almost every Indian religious system and is a practical counterpart of some schools of philosophical thought as well. But in essence, Yoga is independent of both religion and philosophy and is a tool available for serious application anywhere and by anybody. A scientifically trained mind can use it most efficiently once it realizes that there are limits beyond which current methods of scientific research cannot penetrate and that there is a need to go beyond those limits.

Third, the Indian tradition offers man an outlook of a universal redemption which has been the dream of utopian thinking in the West for many centuries, either as a religious expectation of a millennium or in the form of a perfect social order brought about by revolution or social progress or even as a technological paradise ruled by scientists. Compared with these ideals the Indian outlook appears more realistic as well as more attractive. Both paths, the Buddhist and the Hindu, particularly as expressed in the Bodhisattva vow and in Aurobindo's conception of the accomplished man collaborating with the Divine mind on the spiritualization of the world, express the idea that the world can be redeemed only by the effort of individual people who have first made sufficient spiritual progress themselves before they can help others and contribute to the final goal of spiritualization or redemption of the world. Without that conscious effort on the part of a number of individuals the goal will not be reached for it is neither an outcome of inevitable evolution nor a gift from God. The initial responsibility for setting the liberating process in motion rests with man, but this process cannot be completed with merely human forces as we know them: a final happy state of mankind cannot be achieved through technological, economic and social progress alone.

The Indian tradition thus offers modern man a challenge in the form of a discipline which would greatly broaden his horizon and turn his mind from fascination by the senses and the sensory world with all its technological miracles towards the possibility and desirability of a spiritual awakening. By making the three points just described into three pillars of a consciously followed spiritual discipline, man can initiate a process of growth within his personality which will eventually culminate in a spiritual maturity that will make him master of his destiny.

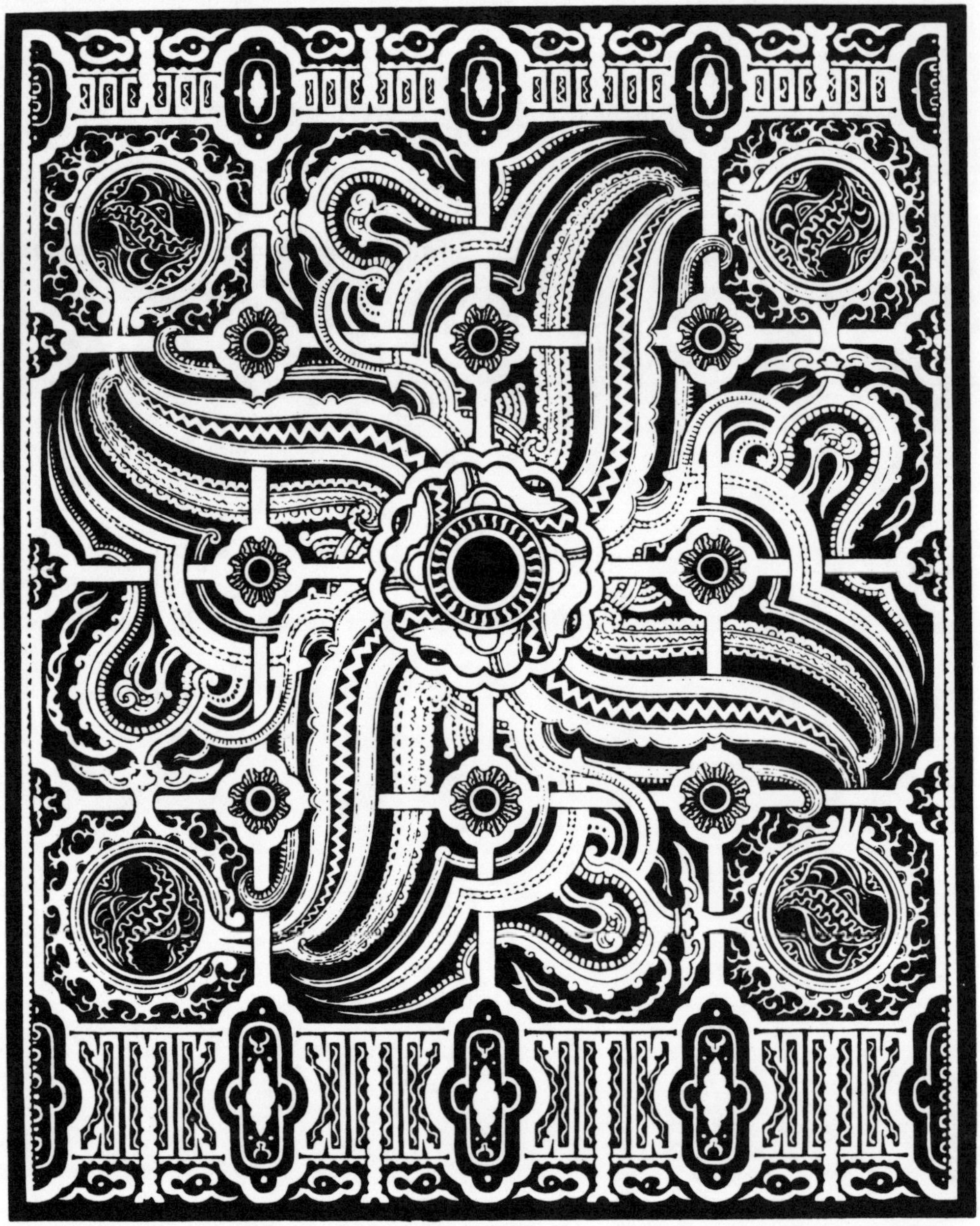

Contents

Vincent Stuart: Preface
Carolyn Rose King: Touching the Earth
Henri Tracol: Thus Spake Beelzebub
Maurice Nicoll: On the Formation of a Psychological Body
Mary C. Fullerson: Discovery of Intimate Order
Z'ev ben Shimon Halevi: Order: A Kabbalistic Approach
Karlfried Graf von Dürckheim: On the Double Origin of Man
Herbert V. Guenther: Towards Spiritual Order
Jean Eracle: The Buddhist Way to Deliverance
John Blofeld: Return to the Source
Karel Werner: Spiritual Personality and its Formation according to Indian Tradition

$4.50

0-394-73350-9